THE FOUNDATIONS OF A FREE SOCIETY

Also by Andrew R. Cecil

The Third Way:
Enlightened Capitalism and the
Search for a New Social Order

The
Foundations
of
a Free
Society

By

Andrew R. Cecil

Supplement to
The Andrew R. Cecil Lectures on Moral Values
in a Free Society

The University of Texas at Dallas
1983

Library of Congress Catalog Card Number 83–051203
International Standard Book Number 0-292-72447-0

Distributed by the University of Texas Press,
Box 7819, Austin, Texas 78712

To my wife
KATE

FOREWORD

The University of Texas at Dallas established the
Andrew R. Cecil Lectures on Moral Values in a Free
Society in 1979. This lecture series stemmed from
the realization that an institution of higher education
has a responsibility that goes beyond those other
essential missions of providing excellent professional preparation for its students and of establishing
an environment where vital research may be carried
out. A university must also provide a forum for the
discussion and debate of the important issues of its
society and time. It was in order to fulfill this responsibility that the Lectures on Moral Values in a Free
Society were made an important part of the life of our
campus.

The Lectures were named for the Distinguished
Scholar in Residence at the University, Dr. Andrew
R. Cecil. After a long and distinguished career in law
and education on three continents, Dr. Cecil came to
the campus of The University of Texas at Dallas as
the President of The Southwestern Legal Foundation when that Foundation made the University its
home. Upon his retirement from the Presidency of
the Foundation—which he continues to serve as
Chancellor Emeritus and Trustee—the University
extended its invitation to him to serve as Distinguished Scholar in Residence and to name the lecture series in his honor.

Dr. Cecil has taken the most active interest in the
series and has been a primary force in assuring its
success. At the request of the University, he deliv-

ered the inaugural series of Lectures in 1979. The proceedings of that series made permanently available as Volume I of the Andrew R. Cecil Lectures on Moral Values in a Free Society, *The Third Way: Enlightened Capitalism and the Search for a New Social Order*. The seven Lectures comprising the book contain Dr. Cecil's analysis of the moral underpinnings of our economic and social order. They address problems as various as dogmas and moral values, economics and Christian ethics, and the striving for self-determination and basic human rights throughout the world. These various strands are united by Dr. Cecil's unfailing insistence on individual dignity and the intrinsic worth of each human being.

A lecture by Dr. Cecil has graced each of the four subsequent series. Because these four addresses, taken as a whole provide an important extension of the ideas and arguments adumbrated in *The Third Way*, the University has thought it would be useful to collect them and publish them as a supplementary volume to the series of published proceedings of the Lectures on Moral Values in a Free Society. This new collection of Dr. Cecil's addresses is fittingly entitled *The Foundations of a Free Society*. This book explores the bedrock on which our liberties are founded: morality and religion, justice and natural rights, knowledge and education. Just as *The Third Way* stressed that there must be a third way far removed from totalitarian control and heedless individualism, *The Foundations of a Free Society* stresses that restraint and responsibility are essential prerequisites to true liberty.

On the occasion of Dr. Cecil's retirement from the Presidency of The Southwestern Legal Foundation, its long-time distinguished Trustee, Mr. James E. O'Brien, paid tribute to him in the following words:

> "In the bewildering array of events, forces, and laws which shape our lives, Andrew Cecil has always sought to state his convictions and philosophy . . . in the broadest terms of human aspirations and verities. From Solon to Solzhenitsyn, from Kant to de Tocqueville (and nearer at home, Thomas Jefferson), he has drawn example and precept.
>
> "Always his speeches, writings, and reports have underscored man's everlasting quest for knowledge, for discipline, for moderation, for free and informed discussion, and for the truth and meaning of human existence."

These words are as fitting today as they were in 1977.

The University owes Andrew R. Cecil a debt of gratitude for the interest he has taken in the Lectures on Moral Values in a Free Society, and for the substantial and important contribution these Lectures represent to the reconsideration of the fundamental values on which our nation is based.

This year marks the fifth series of the Lectures, and the University can look back with pride on the achievement that these Lectures represent. A dozen and a half outstanding scholars and statesmen from all over the nation and, indeed, the world shared the results of their most deeply considered ponderings. All of them of substantial achievement, they have taken stock of their accumulated wisdom and addressed issues of preeminent importance to our society. All of these Lectures have been rich in insight and memorable for all who have heard them. Their range of topics has been prodigious. But all have shared a single focus: the moral foundations of our culture, often assumed but seldom examined in depth. These Lectures help to insure that such foundations are understood and preserved.

This is another pleasant occasion to express our gratitude to the donors who have made the Cecil Lectures possible. Their far-sightedness has enabled the University to establish an important tradition and fulfill our desire to shed light on the moral heritage of our nation.

Robert H. Rutford, President
The University of Texas at Dallas
November 1983

CONTENTS

INTRODUCTION

The term "democracy" was coined in Greece to describe a government where people participate in directing the affairs of the State and in making its laws. Aristotle defines a citizen as "one who is capable of ruling and being ruled in turn," but more in harmony with the facts of Greek history is his definition describing a citizen as "one who has part in judicial decisions, and in holding office." Pure democracy did not exist in Greece. There was always an aristocratic or oligarchic basis for representation in making "judicial decisions, and in holding office." The masses could only claim the power of criticism and judgment of the government's policies and conduct.

Aristotle, the son of a physician, a philosopher and a student of marine biology, as a middle class professional man recognized the importance of the man in the street. He wished, therefore, to combine aristocracy, the essence of which, he thought, is "distribution of offices according to goodness," with the will of majority, which in a democracy should prevail. He saw good government in cities with a large middle class, which has a "great steadying influence and checks the opposing extremes" of the rich and the poor.

Greece remained in a condition of permanent change, and, with each change of constitution, there was a shift in the balance of power. The principle of political compromise and concessions which later frequently prevailed during the history of Rome, was not a feature of most Greek states. In early Rome the basis of political organization was the clan *(gens)*. The patricians had full rights of citizenship. The second class known as *plebs*—formed by *clientes* released from the duties they owed their patrons (the patricians) and by newcomers, who did not attach themselves to the representatives of prominent Roman families—lacked organization, had no part in the management of Rome's affairs, and was denied the civil rights and political privileges of the patricians.

This class discrimination and prejudice in favor of patricians became a source of serious conflicts. The able-bodied plebeians who served in the army and participated in the military expansion of Rome demanded a voice in government. Through compromises and political concessions, the plebeians under the empire made great constitutional gains that ended the patricio-plebeian struggle.

Although under the empire citizenship meant practically the same thing for patricians and plebeians, there gradually came forth into being a second class that comprised those who were outside the privileged classes. This class, known also as *plebs* (but not to be confused with the same term used under the republic) was essentially without political rights, but its members could rise into higher orders by acquiring a fortune required by these higher orders (senatorial and equestrian).

In the medieval ages, the great mass of the less fortunate were bound to service in return for the protection their landlords could provide them. In the feudal structure, where ownership of land became a system of government, we may find the seeds of the

idea of contract binding the rulers and the people
and involving mutual duties. This idea was an important development in the philosophy of democracy.

In England, John Locke in his *Two Treatises of
Government* (1690) exposed the idea of democracy
derived from the social contract and based on natural
law. The social contract, he maintained, vests
sovereignty in the people, who have the right and the
obligation to withdraw their support of a government
that does not comply with the popular will. The
writers of the American Constitution drew heavily
on the theory of law and government expounded by
John Locke by weaving into the very fabric of its
legal order the concepts of Natural Law and Natural
Rights.

From the beginning of the history of our nation, it
has been recognized that a republic is the type of
governance that demands the most from its people in
terms of morality, justice, knowledge, wisdom, and
responsibility. That is why it has been constantly
stressed that only virtue, actively exercised and vigilantly maintained, could preserve the rights and
prerogatives of democracy. The history of the twentieth century gives all too much evidence of the
fragility of democracy and the need for careful
watchfulness over it.

After World War II, we seem to be witnessing on
the international stage the fulfillment of Alexis de
Toqueville's prophecy that two great nations—the
United States and Russia—would some day come to
sway the destinies of the world. Soviet Russia, in its
drive to impose communism on all the world, re-

fused to abide by the sacredness of human rights rooted in the natural moral law, but the Free World seems to hesitate in proclaiming these rights—a failure which inevitably has resulted in a series of surrenders. Encouraged by the hesitation, Soviet Russia expanded its imperialistic right of tyranny to Eastern Europe, invaded and imposed a government of its own choice on the people of Afghanistan, and with tanks and guns shattered the dreams of freedom of nations suffering under the heels of communist regimes.

During this period since World War II, the United States has become the bastion of hope for the Free World. The United States did not gain one inch of new territory in the war, although it was the only undamaged industrial power in the world and had a monopoly of nuclear weapons with the ability to deliver them anywhere. Instead of militaristic expansion, the United States offered the world the Marshall Plan, the Point IV program, and other foreign aid programs to rebuild the war-ravaged economies of the world, including Germany and Japan, who had been our enemies.

These two diametrically different courses of activity of the world powers demonstrate the difference between the policy of dehumanizing barbarism offered by the totalitarian enemies of the Free World and the policy of respect for human rights by assisting nations plunged into the tragedy of war and economic disasters. History shows us, however, that every civilization faces ups and downs and some of the symptoms of civilization in decay are sadly in evidence today in Western civilization. One of the principal concerns of twentieth century historians is the process of decay in the civilizations of Europe and the United States. Unless it is reversed, they warn us, it will bring the West before long to the point that preceded the crumbling of Rome's walls in the fifth century.

Among these historians we shall list Professor Robert Nisbet, who in his book *Twilight of Authority* is concerned by the continued trend toward "a military Leviathan" and "social equalitarianism which is bred less by the moral value of equality than by centralized power's leveling effects upon the natural hierarchies of all social institutions." (Oxford University Press, 1975, p. vi.)

Decline in popular trust of government and its leaders, loss of respect for law, and the decline of forms in all spheres of social and political life; the growing conflict between democracy and bureaucracy; the specter of insecurity caused by the rising volume of crime and the increasing threat or terror; the diminishing ties of race, loyalty, religion, and kinship; the erosion of patriotism and of the sacred in human affairs; disillusionment in state and social order; and the dislocation of the local community are, according to Professor Nisbet, some of the marks of the age in which we live, the age of crumbling social and cultural walls that have protected our Constitution and democracy.

Many share the belief that today our civilization and our nation face the most serious crisis of the century, perhaps of many centuries, and are highly skeptical that the arrest or reversal of the social disintegration around us is possible. We dispute this idea, since we believe that the people of the United States of America are the heirs of a mighty heritage that bears within itself the power to confront and reduce the peril of any such crisis. George Santayana said that "To be an American is of itself almost a moral condition, an education, and a career." Each symptom of a decline in society creates a challenge that should bring forth the best efforts of the society to overcome the danger of decay.

History teaches us that the decay of civilization is not caused by an iron law of fate but results from human failures to establish values which elevate and do not degrade. We must avoid such failures in the future and seek to remedy those of the immediate past. The decay of civilization is not an incurable disease which cannot be prevented; it does not come as a violent shock, like an earthquake. It can be counteracted, because changes in our society are not decreed by nature.

When symptoms of disorder appear, there is no reason to despair. A free society has the ability to shape its destiny. Since the behavior of society is the sum of the behavior of its members—its citizens—it is up to these citizens to understand and preserve the conditions, which secure individual freedom and equal opportunity for all men, as well as responsible government under the rule of law. At the heart of preserving our civilization is the recognition that the civilization which we represent cannot survive materially unless it is redeemed spiritually. Only such recognition can summon us to act, to replace sterile debates by common action that leads to a common understanding of the divergent groups that form a free society and to preserving the heritage of the values instilled in our institutions and our tradition of democracy.

Democracy rests upon a spiritual foundation that led to the establishment in the United States of a separation of the legislative, executive, and judicial branches of government, a harmonious arrangement with an accountability for the performance of our governmental agencies. On this foundation rests our political and civil freedoms, which permit participation in the affairs of government, which establish the right to speak and worship without fear, which make torture and governmental misconduct alien to the experience of every citizen, and which assure social justice, equity and due process for all.

People desire to live in a decent, law-abiding free society, and the crux of their aspirations is understanding human nature. Because of the importance of understanding the true meaning of life and of the need of a public philosophy of civility, our forefathers recognized that religion, morality, and knowlege are necessary to good government. This recognition is as valid today as it was when the government of the Northwest Territory declared in the Ordinance of 1787 that "religion, morality and knowledge being necessary to good government and the happiness of mankind, schools and the means of education shall forever be encouraged."

A free society is a society with established values of respect for the dignity and worth of our fellowman, of concern for individual self-realization, and of appreciation of the imperatives of justice.

The conviction that justice is of supreme importance dominates the prophecy of Amos, the shepherd from the village of Tekoa, whose prophetic outlook can only be compared with those of Isaiah and Jeremiah. As for all the great Hebrew prophets, the essential point for Amos is that all nations are subject to one law and rule. Since God is the Creator of the entire world, His rule extends to all events that take place in its farthest corners. When man rebels against the rule of God by a lack of concern about the miseries experienced by his fellowman, by taking advantage of the weak, or by malpractice in the market and in the courts, oppression and inequity appear. In understanding the relation of obedience to God, justice in political life and economic affairs is as important—or perhaps more important—as worship.

Amos, like Isaiah and Jeremiah, denounces those who by means of religious rite seek to cover over their transgressions and the perversion of the principle of justice. For the worshippers at Bethel and Gilgal he gives the warning:

> "I hate, I despise your feasts, and I take no delight in your solemn assemblies. Even though you offer me your burnt offerings and cereal offerings, I will not accept them, and the peace offerings of your fatted beasts I will not look upon. Take away from me the noise of your songs; to the melody of your harps I will not listen. But let justice roll down like waters, and righteousness like an ever-flowing stream." (Amos 5:21-24.)

Justice is thought by philosophers to be the greatest of virtues, and as Aristotle described it,

"Neither evening nor morning star is so wonderful."
The "just" cannot be equated with the "legal." Justice in the judicial sense, which expresses the letter
of the law, is epitomized by the blindfold on the eyes
of the statute emblemizing the virtue. It calls for
conformity to the laws that are established. But every
government is a government of men, and the judges
who constitute the courts are also men. The courts
are no wiser or better than the judges who constitute
them. Furthermore, the so-called "rule of law" does
not sustain itself; each generation reshapes its forms
and rekindles its values in the light of its own experience.

Spinoza warned that "he who tries to fix and determine everything by law inflames rather than corrects the vices of the world." The concept of law is
clouded when eternal moral principles are not understood. The history of mankind is the history of the
search to discover the immediate higher law of divine origin. The moral order was revealed to man
through reason, and through reason man can discern
and participate in the divine plan of creation and in
discovering the sense of justice which dictates to him
what is right or wrong, just or unjust.

Natural justice is a sense of justice attained by the
light of reason essentially agreeable with the constitution of human nature and of a free society. This
sense of justice has an all-important influence upon
the desire to search out and apply the rules appropriate to a free society. It goes beyond mere technical
legal rights covered by the letter of the law. As Justice Oran M. Roberts described it, "It is like the polar

star that guides the voyager, although it may not stand over the port of destination."

Justice is concerned with the acts of the government and its rightful exercise of the authority necessary to maintain an orderly organized society. *The Federalist*, described by Jefferson as "the best commentary on the principle of government which was ever written," in its emphasis on the role of government makes the following statement: "A good government implies two things: first, fidelity to the object of government, which is happiness of the people, secondly, a knowledge of the means by which the object can be best obtained." *(Federalist 62.)* One of the means is the right to "due process of law" that rests on the Fifth and Fourteenth Amendments.

Reinhold Niebuhr wrote: "Man's capacity for justice makes democracy possible, but man's inclination to injustice makes democracy necessary." To paraphrase this statement we may say that man's or government's inclination to injustice makes due process of law necessary. Although "due process" has never achieved a precise meaning, it serves as a means of social control by safeguarding us against the possibilities of executive, legislative, or military tyranny. It has been defined as the very essence of a scheme of ordered justice. The due process clause is not limited to the protection of fairness of procedures. With all proper procedures meticulously followed (procedural due process), due process also protects against arbitrary, unreasonable, and capricious actions by government (substantive due process).

The very nature of due process negates any concept of inflexible standards applicable to every imaginable situation. It depends on circumstances, and its purpose is to ensure the fair and orderly administration of the laws to protect our fundamental rights against federal or state encroachment. Justice Brandeis in his dissent in the *Olmstead* case explained:

> "Decency, security, and liberty alike demand that government officials shall be subjected to the same rules of conduct that are commands to the citizen. In a government of laws, existence of the government will be imperiled if it fails to observe the law scrupulously. Our government is the potent, the omnipresent teacher. For good or for ill, it teaches the whole people by its example." *(Olmstead v. United States,* 277 U.S. 438, 485, 48 S.Ct. 570, 575 [1927].)

The communist regimes from their inception adopted a policy of lying to their people and of covering up the realities of the outside world to avoid any comparisons. Since there must always be a scapegoat for the failures of a planned economy, the only way of escaping sanctions by those responsible for carrying out the plan is to provide the government with spurious reports and inflated figures. The Soviet population, wrote Alexander Solzhenitsyn, has only one way of resisting their enslavement, "it steals, in turn, its daily bread from the government .... Many items—wire, nails, machine oil, paint, fertilizer—simply cannot be purchased honestly anywhere in the country, but they can be stolen at one's place of employment and then sold on the black market." Concluded Solzhenitsyn: "Communism is a denial of life: it is a fatal disease of a nation and the death of all humanity. And there is no nation on earth that has immunity against Communism." *(National Review,* January 21, 1983, pp. 33, 34.)

We agree that communism is a disease that cannot be remedied, but we do not agree with the position that no country can be immune from it. Modern society has the ability to shape its destiny. To win the global war of ideas and to remain free, we will have to win the battle for the mind and the spirit. The responsibility for the preservation of our liberty, of justice, and of equality under the law is shared by all citizens, and most of all by our educational institutions.

In the battle for the minds of men, it is refreshing to recall Woodrow Wilson's advice: "The only thing that is worthwhile in human intercourse, after all, is to wake somebody up, provided you wake them up to see the light, provided you wake them up to see something that is worth seeing and to comprehend something that their spirits have not hitherto comprehended." Study of basic concepts of a free society serves to uplift the moral thinking of our young men and women, thus preparing them to discharge their moral obligations as citizens.

CHAPTER I

MORALITY, RELIGION, AND KNOWLEDGE: ESSENTIAL COMPONENTS OF HARMONY IN GOVERNMENT

The Establishment Clause

Moral values are an indispensable part of human life, and morality has relevance to every decision made in the life of a man or a nation. These values may not always be clearly articulated, but they are there, determining which of the several alternatives facing us will lead toward evil or toward the common good. When moral guidance as a basis of action is overlooked in favor of other forces molding human events, the usefulness or even the possibility of defining the ultimate worth of human beings is denied. The result is an impoverishment of the spiritual heritage of a nation and a dangerous heedlessness in its public life.

In 1955, Walter Lippmann decried the growing disorder in the public life of Western civilization that grew out of the neglect and denial of the moral values that underlay the founding of this country. Convinced that there is a "body of positive principles and precepts which a good citizen cannot deny or ignore," he wrote, "I believe there is a public philosophy. Indeed there is such a thing as a public philosophy of civility. It does not have to be discovered or invented. It is known. But it does have to be revived and renewed." (*The Public Philosophy*, Little, Brown and Company, 1955, p. 101.) Lippmann located this philosophy in the tradition of natural law, a position I defended in my book *The Third Way*.

That there is indeed a public philosophy of civility that provides a moral grounding for all our institutions was assumed by our forefathers, even before the formal birth of our nation. The Ordinance of 1787 for the government of the Northwest Territory declared that "religion, morality, and knowledge being necessary to good government and the happiness of mankind, schools and the means of education shall forever be encouraged." In our day, when all too often the practical ends of education are stressed, it is inspiring to look back on this rationale for the public fostering of education. In the interpretation of the Ordinance, the courts held that true religion includes true morality and that all that is comprehended in the words "religion and morality" and can be the subject of human instruction must be included under the general term "knowledge." Since knowledge is the "hand-maid of virtue," religion and morality are aided and promoted by the increase and diffusion of knowledge.

The Ordinance was followed by the adoption of the Constitution of the United States. It is the First Amendment to our Constitution which states that "Congress shall make no law respecting an establishment of religion" and is thus known as the establishment clause. Strengthened by the Fourteenth Amendment, which made the establishment clause applicable to the states, the First Amendment has been one of the great pillars of American liberties. But it is important to distinguish between the proper effects of that amendment and those effects that were not intended by the drafters of the Bill of Rights. The proper effects include legal separation of church and State as well as the religious liberty which is such a great part of the American heritage. Among the effects that were not intended is the attempt to bar the search for ultimate truth or preclude the application of religious and moral principles to public life.

The first and most immediate purpose of the adoption of the First Amendment was the belief that a union of government and religion tends to destroy government and degrade religion. "United with government, religion never rises above the merest superstition; united with religion, government never rises above the merest despotism; and all history shows us that the more widely and completely they are separated the better it is for both." *(Board of Education of Cincinnati v. Minor,* 23 Ohio St. 211, 13 Am. Rep. 233 [1872].) This separation of the domains of government and religion was designed to give each realm its proper place in the lives of the citizens of our country.

Our Founding Fathers strove to find the proper expression for their desire to protect both government and religion from mutual interference. In opposition to the bill establishing provision for teachers of the Christian religion introduced in 1784 in the House of Delegates of the State of Virginia, James Madison prepared the widely circulated "Memorial and Remonstrance," in which he demonstrated "that religion, or the duty we owe the

Creator" was not within the cognizance of civil government. The proposed bill was defeated, and another drafted by Thomas Jefferson was passed.

Jefferson's bill "for establishing religious freedom" defines that freedom in its preamble. After stating that "to suffer the civil magistrate to intrude his powers into the field of opinion and to restrain the profession or propagation of principles on supposition of their ill tendency is a dangerous fallacy which at once destroys all religious liberty," the Act declared that "it is time enough, for the rightful purposes of civil government, for its officers to interfere when principles break out into overt acts against peace and good order." In these two sentences, stated the Supreme Court of the United States, "is found the true distinction between what properly belongs to church and what to the state." (*Reynolds v. United States*, 98 U.S. 145, 163, 25 L. Ed. 244 [1878].)

The First Amendment to the Constitution forbids legislation that will prohibit the free exercise of religion, thus guaranteeing religious freedom. Belief in religious freedom and in the separation of church and State does not, however, preclude the conviction that the three qualities discussed in the Northwest Territory Ordinance—morality, religion, and knowledge—are essential components of good government. The search for truth and for a basis of actions that will promote the common good calls for scholarly and critical examination of the basic concepts of religious faith, of moral value systems, and of facts and experiences offered by mankind's knowledge.

To pursue such examination we have to define morality and religion—terms which countless philosophers and scholars for many generations have sought to define. In search for definitions we shall endeavor to analyze the principal values that morality and religion have in satisfying human yearnings. The critical questions to be answered are: What is the common ground between morality and religion? Have all systems of morality religious roots? To what extent have attempts to repudiate the religious roots of a moral system succeeded in creating conflict and to what extent have faith and the values that are enshrined in religious traditions brought harmony to the world? To answer these questions it is imperative to define morality and religion.

Morality Defined

Jesus, when asked by Pilate whether He was a king, replied, "My task is to bear witness to the truth. For this was I born; for this I came into the world, and all who are not deaf to truth listen to my voice." To which Pilate retorted, "What is truth?" (John 18:37-38.) Scholars have not yet agreed on the answer to Pilate's question. Morality, like truth, belongs to a group of terms that includes values such as religion, justice, beauty, and conscience, which have a great impact on human life.

In searching for the substance of these terms, however, we are confronted with a great variety of definitions often conflicting with one another, because some of them are too narrow and others too exhaustive. To demonstrate the difficulty of defining

the nature of morality because of the diverse views of
the theorists, we shall examine the contrasting concepts of morality embodied in the philosophies of
two giants in the history of ethics, Plato and Aristotle.
These two philosophers lived in the same period and
represented the same Greek tradition. Indeed,
Aristotle even began as a pupil of Plato. Although we
might expect to find essential agreement, instead we
find a great discrepancy in these two philosophers'
ideas of morality.

In the Greek tradition, the inquiries of both Plato
and Aristotle and the theories which developed from
their teaching are directed toward discovering the
nature of human happiness—toward search for the
"good life." Both believe that reason is the highest
part of man's nature and that the life which accords
with reason is the happiest life. The ultimate knowledge upon which moral virtue is based is the knowledge of "good." According to Plato, "good" is the
universal author of all things beautiful and right,
independent of circumstances and human experience:

> "[I]n the world of knowledge the idea of good
> appears last of all, and is seen only with an effort;
> and when seen, is also inferred to be universal
> author of all things beautiful and right, parent of
> light and the lord of light in this visible world, and
> the immediate source of reason and truth in the
> intellectual. . . ."

Plato is absorbed in mental abstraction, in a subjective future. Aristotle, on the other hand, is a

realist, resolved to concern himself with the objective present, with the external presence of reality. He agrees with Plato that the "good" for man is happiness, but insists that this basic moral principle is inherent in our activities and that it can be discovered through their study, although opinions about its nature may differ. The "good" we are seeking is different, for instance, in medicine, in military strategy, in architecture, or in any other realm of human endeavor. In medicine it is health, in military strategy victory, in architecture a building both useful and beautiful—"for it is for the sake of this that all men do whatever else they do." Some find happiness in pleasure, others in wealth or recognition, because men differ from one another and often even the same man identifies "good" with different things: with health when he is ill or with wealth when he is poor. Aristotle disagrees with Plato that apart from these many "goods" there is another "good" which is self-subsistent and above our comprehension and cause the "goodness" we are able to observe, study, and comprehend.

The name "man," for instance, has a universal application to all members of the human race, but the universal man exists only in our thoughts, he does not exist in reality. We are surrounded, maintains Aristotle, not with universal generic man but with specific individuals, present in reality. In his view, *nomina* (names) should be distinguished from *res* (things); hence comes the clash between the nominalists and the realists. This conflict between the nominalists—the followers of Plato—and the realists—the followers of Aristotle—runs so deep throughout the history of philosophy that the German philosopher Friedrich von Schlegel (1772-1829), the originator of the Romantic school of thought, remarked, "every man is born either a Platonist or an Aristotelian."

The contrasting views of Plato and Aristotle on the nature of the ultimate moral principle should perhaps discourage the attempt to define morality, yet we are driven on by Voltaire's warning, "If you wish to converse with me, define the terms." It may well be profitable to conduct our search on a more mundane plane than that of the Greek philosophers. According to common understanding, the term "morality" or "morals" refers to the common sense of the community, its sense of decency, propriety, and respect for established ideas and institutions, among other things. In a legal context, Benjamin Cardozo defined the moral standards of the community as the "norm or standard of behavior which struggles to make itself articulate in law." *(Paradoxes of Legal Science,* New York, Columbia University Press, 1928, pp. 17, 41-42.) Morality has also been referred to as synonymous with character *(Warkentin v. Kleinwachter,* 166 Okla. 218, 27 P.2d 160 [1933]), or as a generic term, containing the sum total of moral traits, including honesty, fidelity, peacefulness, and so on. *(State v. Moorman,* 321 P.2d 236, 240, 133 Mont. 148]1958].)

Because of the countless meanings which scholars have given to this term—some pointless to our dicussion—and at the risk of some simplification, we define morality as the aggregate of rules and principles which relate to man's right or wrong conduct and prescribe the standards or norms by which man guides and controls his actions in his dealings with others.

Consideration of the conditions requisite to the fulfillment of man's moral duties leads into discussions of the terms "ethics" and "conscience." While jurisprudence deals with actions in their relation to law, for the most part independently of a consideration of motives, it is the province of ethics to examine the relationship between actions and the motives behind them. Ethics has thus been defined as "the science of the moral," as "moral philosophy," or as "the study of standards of conduct and of moral judgment."

The word "moral" derives from the Latin word *mores* and "ethics" from the Greek word *ethos;* both source-words refer to traditional human behavior. The word "ethics" is most often used in reference to professional conduct. A professional code of ethics is generally understood as the accepted standard of professional people in busines relations peculiar to their professional employment. Such a code is the consensus of expert opinion as to necessary standards within a profession.

The courts have taken the position that in the general treatment of professional ethics sometimes so much stress has been put on the adjective "professional" that the substantive "ethics" has been lost sight of. It should rather be understood that "there is no difference between personal and professional ethics." (*In re Williams*, 50 P.2d 729, 732, 174 Okla. 386 [1935].)

Conscience

Because of the manifold and often contradictory connotations of the word "conscience," the theologian Richard Rothe suggests that we exclude this term from the scientific treatment of ethics. Conscience, however, plays such an important part in our discussion of the role of morality in public life that we cannot fail to consider what it is and what its function should be. Moral scientists explain conscience as the "moral sense" which gives us the power to distinguish between right and wrong. According to some moralists, conscience connotes a form of intuition. To the British philospher Anthony Shaftesbury is attributed the term "moral sense"—man's natural sense of right and wrong in a universe which is essentially harmonious. Another British philosopher and theologian, Ralph Cudworth, representing the seventeenth-century group called the Cambridge Platonists, argued that moral ideas are innate in man.

In the eighteenth century, the British philosopher and clergyman Bishop Joseph Butler saw the springs of all human action in two of the principles which regulate man's behavior, benevolence and self-love. The natural principle of *benevolence*, he wrote, "is in some degree to *society*, what *self-love* is to the *individual* . . . though the former tends most directly to public good, and the latter to private: yet they are so perfectly coincident that the greatest satisfactions to ourselves depend upon our having benevolence in a due degree; and that self-love is one chief security of our right behaviour toward society."

There is no natural opposition between these two principles, according to Butler, because of another principle in man that reflects upon his own nature, that approves, disapproves, or remains indifferent to our actions. This principle in man, "by which he approves or disapproves his heart, temper, and actions, is conscience." In one form or another this principle of reflection, inner perception, or conscience is regarded as important by those moral philosophers known as intuitionists. Foremost among them is Immanuel Kant, who in his revolutionary metaphysical system accepted a universal moral law as pragmatically necessary. Kant called the supreme moral principle which man ought to follow the "categorical imperative," the unconditional command of the conscience: "Act as if the maxim from which you act were to become through your will a universal law of nature." The moral imperative is absolute and the moral sense innate, not derived from questionable self-experience; we act in obedience to this inner sense of duty, to these *a priori* principles of morals that command our behavior.

Opposed to this idea is the theory advocated by the empiricists, who hold that there is no moral faculty as such which distinguishes between right and wrong, but that all our knowledge comes from experience and through our senses. John Locke denied the existence of innate ideas of right and wrong, ideas inherited in the mind from birth, inborn in every human soul. He taught that a man enters the world not equipped with ideas but with a mind that is a clean sheet—a *tabula rasa*. Sense-experience begets ideas of right and wrong, and moral judgment comes from man's voluntary actions with regard to human or divine law.

According to Spinoza, conscience is the deposit of the moral traditions of the group and varies with geography; it is not innate but acquired. Thomas Hobbes makes a distinction between the public conscience, which is the law of the commonwealth, and private conscience. He rejects any thoughts that every private man is to be the judge of good or evil as "diseases of a commonwealth, that proceed from the poison of seditious doctrines." This doctrine, he states, is "directly against the essence of a commonwealth." Evaluations of good and evil are transient, vary from occasion to occasion, and are relative to the individual.

The study of human evolution has in some measure brought about a reconciliation of the two conflicting theories we have been discussing. Acceptance of the doctrine of organic evolution, according to the nineteenth-century British philosopher Herbert Spencer, determines certain ethical conceptions. Conscience, like everything else, has evolved and, through the process of adaptation to the ends of life, has become the product of age-long experience. By admitting also that certain moral conceptions may have become hereditary with the individual, Spencer reconciles the intuitionists and the empiricists. Harmony in a society can be obtained through the application of the formula of justice, which, Spencer believes, should be: "Every man is free to do that which he wills provided he infringes not the equal freedom of any other man." This formula is conformable to the belief that there is an inborn moral sense, as well as to the ideas of those representing the evolutionary view. It frees the individual from aggression, protects his right to life, liberty, and the pursuit of happiness on equal terms with all and also permits each individual—through natural selection—to prosper according to his ability and willingness to work.

Whenever the belief in a moral sense is weakened by a loss of respect for the law, a rising volume of crime, an increasing threat of terror, acts of aggression, or atrocities of war, we should be reminded of the sentiments of honesty, generosity, sympathy, paternal love, and other impulses of altruism that strengthen and undergird this belief. Thomas Jefferson asserted that "morality, compassion, generosity are innate elements of the human condition." Without such forces at work in the heart of man, we may as well give up our hopes for a free and civilized community.

In answering the question "What is conscience?" our courts have taken the position that every man of ordinary intelligence understands, in whatever words he may express it, that conscience is that moral sense which dictates to him right or wrong. This sense may differ in degree in individual members of society, but no reasonable being, whether controlled by it or not in his conduct, is wholly destitute of it. "Greatly enlightened it is in some by reason of superior education, quickened in others because of settled religious belief in future accountability, dulled in others by vicious habits, but never altogether absent in any." (*Miller v. Miller*, 41 A. 277, 280, 187 Pa. 572 [1898].)

This moral sense led the Greek poet of the New Comedy, Menander (342-291? B.C.), to state, "Conscience is a God to all mortals," and almost twenty-two-hundred years later moved the English poet William Wordsworth to characterize "duty" as the "stern daughter of the Voice of God." This moral sense impelled Martin Luther to nail his theses on the door of the church at Wittenberg and, when he was summoned before the Emperor Charles and the Diet at Worms, gave him strength to hold his ground and to pronounce the historic words, so often quoted, "I neither can nor will recant anything, since it is neither right nor safe to act against conscience. Here I stand. I cannot do other. God help me. Amen."

The "moral sense" is a source of our moral obligations—obligations arising from the admonitions of conscience, out of a state of facts appealing to a universal sense of justice and fairness—which cannot be enforced by legal action but which are binding in conscience and according to natural justice. It is more than acknowledgement of gratitude or a desire to do charity. The court distinguishes gratitude and charity from a moral obligation as follows: "It is an obligation which, though lacking any foundation cognizable in law, springs from a sense of justice and equity, that an honorable person would entertain, but not from a mere sense of doing benevolence or charity." (*State ex rel. Holmes v. Krueger*, 271 Wis. 129, 137, 72 N.W.2d 734, 738 [1955].)

Legal actions are not always accepted as moral by certain segments of our society. Pope Pius IX in 1869 decreed that the soul enters the egg at conception. When the Supreme Court declared abortion legal, the National Conference of Catholic Bishops declared two days later on January 25, 1973, "Although as a result of the Court decision abortion may be legally permissible, it is still morally wrong, and no Court opinion can change the law of God prohibiting the taking of innocent human life. Therefore, as religious leaders, we cannot accept the Court's judgment and we urge people not to follow its reasoning or conclusions."

There is also an important distinction between conscience and principle. Conscience, considered by some philosophers as an original faculty of our nature, springs from an internal source of self-knowledge that decides what is right and wrong, bows to no supeior human authority, is governed by no man-made laws, is unaccountable to human tribunals, and rests alone with its possessor. Principle is the result of judgment, tested by reason, and yields to the decision of an intelligent mind in approving or condemning our actions.

There may be no connection between conscience and principle. A man may be opposed on principle to what he conscientiously believes to be right. One example may be capital punishment. To quote one decision of our courts: "Many men are opposed on principle to capital punishment, because as often remarked, they believe that the worst use that can be made of a man is to hang him; they believe that society would be benefited by the adoption of some other mode of punishment, and yet, as long as the law provides that certain crimes shall be punished with death, would feel no conscientious scruples in finding a verdict of guilty against one accused of such a crime." *(The People v. Stewart*, 7 Cal. 140,141 [1857].) The situation, we believe, is different with the man who opposes the death penalty from considerations of conscience—he opposes the infliction of death as contrary to the laws of nature, of God, and of the rule of right.

We may be opposed in principle to negotiations with extortionists and kidnappers, yet feel no conscientious scruples when such negotiations to save the victims of criminal acts take place and ransom is paid, even when the act of terrorism is performed by a foreign government. We may be opposed in principle to interference in the domestic affairs of small nations, yet feel no conscientious scruples when the purpose of the interference—subordinated to prudent consideration—is to counter the intervention of another foreign power when the smaller nation offers an unfriendly foreign power military bases or when it pursues policies that endanger our vital strategic and economic interests.

Freedom of Conscience

The ancient Egyptians and Jews did not have an articulated concept of the individual conscience. They saw as inherent in God's order a system of collective virtues, rewards, and punishments. In the Old Testament, although we find a sense of sin among the Hebrews ("For I know my transgressions, and my sin is ever before me. Against thee, thee only, have I sinned and done that which is evil in thy sight." [Psalm 51:3-4]), there are no direct references to the notion of conscience as such. Yet we do find many examples of the workings of conscience. In the first chapters of the book of Genesis, both Adam and Cain are confronted with the reality of their sins by the voice of God Himself. David is brought to repentance by the accusations of the prophet Nathan. The entire book of Job is devoted to the story of an attempt to reconcile Job's conscience—which is clear of any sense of wrongdoing—with the apparent punishments that have been visited upon him. In the end, Job's assertions of his own innocence are silenced by the vision of the power of God.

The New Testament refers on several occasions to conscience as an element of human nature, as a witness to the law written on human hearts and to man's knowledge of natural law and its moral principles. "When Gentiles who do not possess the law carry out its precepts by the light of nature, then, although they have no law, they are their own law, for they display the effect of the law inscribed on their hearts. Their conscience is called as witness, as their own thoughts argue the case on either side, against them or even for them." (Romans 2:14-15.) Moral conscience as a witness of faith is stressed in Hebrews 9:9 ("According to this arrangement, gifts and sacrifices are offered which cannot perfect the conscience of the worshipper.") and in I Timothy 1:10-20 ("So fight gallantly, armed with faith and a good conscience. It was through spurning conscience that certain persons made shipwreck of their faith."). Thus the New Testament amplified the idea of conscience that it inherited from the Jews and the Greek philosophers by asserting the unique pesonality of each individual and the immortality of his soul.

An individual's judgment may not always be correct, yet he has to follow his conscience, even if
objectively it is an erring one Freedom of conscience
is paramount to all human activities. It is more important than subjection of the moral personality to an
objective truth. In the fourteenth chapter of his
Epistle to the Romans, Paul spells out the obligations of a man to his conscience, since the primary
principle is that no one should act with an uneasy
conscience. This emphasis on the freedom of conscience gave birth to the ideas of inalienable rights,
of the rule of a law that can be invoked against the
State, and of the maxim that governmental authority
must always be kept in check. This maxim proclaims
that a person is more than a political pawn enjoying
only the privileges bestowed on him by the State.
This maxim also proclaims that freedom of conscience is a source of moral power that is higher than
the claims of the State.

Salus Populi

The freedom that conscience demands is not,
however, absolute. This liberty does not altogether
supersede the operation of the principle *salus populi
suprema est lex*—the welfare of the people is the
highest law. This principle is expressly recognized
in the constitutions of many states. Article 38 of the
New York Constitution of 1777, for instance, provides: "[T]he liberty of conscience hereby granted
shall not be so construed as to excuse acts of licentiousness or justify practices inconsistent with the
peace or safety of this State." The same limitation is

repeated in the constitution of 1812 and in that of 1846, and parallels may readily be found in the constitutions of other states.

Our courts consider that the peace and good order of the community must prevail over conscience wherever the community's mental or physical health is affected. This category is a broad one and defers the dictates of individual scruples to the physical examination of school children and of prospective brides and bridegrooms, to the exclusion of obscenity, to vaccination to prevent epidemics, to elimination of drug addiction, and to suppression of mail frauds and other schemes.

The peace and good order of the community must prevail over conscience whenever the violation of generally accepted moral standards of the community makes a breach of the peace reasonably foreseeable. Because of the violation of the community's sense of reverence in a monogamous civilization, legislation punishing polygamy was upheld, even though the Mormons conscientiously believed that their religion sanctioned and commended that practice. Polygamy could, in the courts' opinions, arouse passions leading to breaches of the peace. As mentioned earlier, one of the rightful purposes of civil government, according to Jefferson, is "to interfere when principles break out into overt acts against peace and good order."

Peace and good order must also prevail over conscience when the defense of the country is imperiled. The principles of *salus* is not limited to maintaining the well-being of citizens within their own communiy but extends to protecting the community from exterior agression. In seeking to balance *salus populi* and individual conscience, one of the most widely discussed conflicts is that between scruples concerning the bearing of arms and the safety of the nation. From the inception of the republic, religious objectors have been expressly or implicitly exempt from bearing arms. Claims based solely on disbelief in war as an instrument of human policy have been disallowed by our courts, and only those who objected to service in war because of religious scruples have been exempted. Conscientious scruples concerning economic support of governmental activities have received no encouragement whatsoever by the courts. Since the state's existence has material foundations other than the martial one, conscience cannot be used as a reason for tax avoidance.

Even though the freedom of conscience is not, therefore, absolute, the fact remains that this freedom is the crowning glory of American liberties. It gives to each person the untrammeled and unquestionable right to worship God according to the dictates of his own conscience, without interference from any person or from any source. In the cause of religion, man is prepared to act and to suffer beyond all other causes. History instructs us that many men have died or suffered worse than death for the right to worship according to their consciences. Daniel Webster pointed out that the freedom which conscience demands and the love of religious liberty form a compound sentiment—made up of the dearest sense of right and the highest conviction of duty— which "is able to look the sternest despotism in the face." ("Speech in Commemoration of the First Settlement in New England," Plymouth, 1820.)

Lord Mansfield, one of the most illustrious luminaries of the common law, declared in a famous speech in the case of *Evans v. Chamberlain of London:* "Conscience is not controllable by human laws, nor amenable to human tribunals; persecution or attempts to force conscience will never produce conviction, and were only calculated to make hypocrites or martyrs." Whenever laws have been enacted to force conscience, bloodshed and confusion have resulted because, "There is certainly nothing more unreasonable, nor inconsistent with the rights of human nature, more contrary to the spirit and precepts of the Christian religion, more iniquitous or unjust, more impolitic than persecution against natural religion, revealed religion, and sound polity."

The first legislators to establish religious freedom, Lord Baltimore and William Penn—one a Roman Catholic and the other a Friend—by passing their memorable laws in favor of liberty of conscience and religious freedom secured two of the highest privileges of the human race. These liberties do not diminish the claim of morality and religion or the individual conscience. The tie between morality and religion was stressed by George Washington when he remarked in his Farewell Address:

"Religion and morality are indispensable supports . . . great Pillars of human happiness . . . the firmest props of the duties of men and citizens . . . And let us with caution indulge the supposition, that morality can be maintained without religion.

Whatever may be conceded to the influence of refined education on minds of peculiar structure, reason and experience both forbid us to expect that national morality can prevail in exclusion of religious principle."

This leads to the question: Is morality always rooted in religious faith? To answer this question, we have to define religion and to classify the moral traditions by the values which they consider most important.

Religion Defined

Benjamin Franklin, though often cited as an unbeliever, thought of Christianity as the best religion for the mere purposes of civil government. In his letter to Ezra Stiles, the President of Yale University, in 1790, Franklin called Christianity the "best system of religion and morals the world ever saw or is like to see." On a similar note, our courts have expressed the view that Christianity "is the purest system of morality, the firmest auxiliary, and only support of all human laws." (*Updegraph v. Commonwealth,* 11 Serg. 394, 406 [Pa. 1824].)

Yet the founders of this country and the courts have repeatedly stressed that in any action a magistrate takes in regard to the belief or disbelief of religious principles there is always the danger of trampling on the rights of conscience and of destroying religious liberty. God is the only arbiter and sovereign Lord of conscience and to Him alone man is accountable. The courts of law are not the *forum conscientiae* or *custodes morum* (conservators of morals) and, therefore, have no jurisdiction over "crimes against God" unless they are by necessary consequence crimes against civil society, either consisting of an actual breach of the peace or liable to provoke or excite such a breach. Even in this case, our courts have explained that "we have no right to interfere one inch further than is necessary to prevent outrage and infractions of the peace."

Those who wrote our Constitution never sought to make proselytes by coercion. Whenever the Christian religion is offended without licentiousness endangering the public peace, the courts should leave Christianity to fight her own battles because, "Christianity requires no aid from force or persecution; she asks not to be guarded by fines and forfeitures. She stands secure in her armour of truth and reason. She seeks not to establish her principles by political aid and legal enactments. She seeks mildly and peaceably to establish them in the hearts of the people." *(The State v. Chandler,* 2 Harr. Del 533 [1829].)

Religion does not need an alliance with the State to encourage its growth nor laws to enforce it. Christianity, as the Supreme Court of Illinois reminded us, "had its beginning and grew under oppression. Where it has depended upon the sword of civil authority for its enforcement it has been the weakest. Its weapons are moral and spiritual and its power is not dependent upon the force of majority. It asks from the civil government only impartial protection and concedes to every other sect and religion the same impartial civil right." *(People ex rel. Ring et al. v. Board of Education of Dist. 24,* 245 Ill. 334 [1924].)

What religion is right is not a question to be determined by a court in a country which enjoys religious freedom, but since the Constitution of the United States does not contain a definition of religion, our courts of necessity have defined religion. Without such a definition, the court could not assure the enforcement of the First Amendment, which demands that Congress shall make no law respecting the establishment of religion or forbidding the free exercise thereof. Without such a definition, religion could not be distinguished from cults or particular sects, which—as the recent events in Guyana demonstrated—may have as their tenet human sacrifices on special occasions or advocate promiscuous intercourse of the sexes as prompted by the passions of their members and leaders.

A definition by our highest court is found in the case of *Davis v. Beason* (133 U.S. 333, 342, 10 S. Ct. 299, 300, 33 L. Ed. 637 [1890].): "The term 'religion' has reference to one's views of his relations to his Creator, and to the obligations they inspire of reverence for his being and character, and of obedience to his will. It is often confounded with the *cultus* or form of worship of a particcular sect, but it is distinguishable from the latter." Our courts have promulgated what has been referred to as a "minimum definition." We may also find quoted in court opinions some definitions offered by religious philosophers, such as: "Religion is squaring human life with superhuman life . . . What is common to all religions is belief in a superhuman power and an adjustment of human activities to the requirements of that power, such adjustment as may enable the individual believer to exist more happily." (E. Washburn Hopkins, *The History of Religions,* New York, The Macmillan Company, 1918, p. 2.) Or, religion is "a propitiation or conciliation of powers superior to man which are believed to direct and control the course of nature and of human life." (J.G. Frazer, *The Golden Bough,* One Volume Edition, New York, The Macmillan Company, 1951, pp. 57-58.)

Laws are made to maintain peace and order, and while they cannot interfere with mere religious belief and opinions, they may interfere with religious practices. Can man excuse his practices which violate existing laws because of his religious belief? To permit this, stated the Supreme Court in the case of *Reynolds v. United States,* "would be to make the professed doctrine of religious belief superior to the law of the land, and in effect to permit every citizen to become a law unto himself. Government could exist only in name under such circumstances." (98 U.S. 145, 25 L. Ed. 244 [1878].) As Mr. Justice Cardozo pointed out: "One who is a martyr to principle—which may turn out in the end to be a delusion or an error—does not prove by his martyrdom that he has kept within the law." *(Hamilton v. Regents of University of California,* 298 U.S. 245, 55 S. Ct. 197, 206, 79 L. Ed. 343 [1934].) Crimes are not less odious because sanctioned or asserted to be a part of the religious doctrine advocated by a particular sect that denigrates them as a part of religious nature.

The courts have defined religion only of necessity, because no attempt to define religion in a satisfactory way can be crowned with success. The content of the term "religion" is incapable of compression into a few words or sentences. It is found throughout the history of the human race, common to man in the most primitive and in the most highly developed modern societies. Because it has to do with the entirely personal nature of the experience, belief, and performance of every human being, it is subject to the widest diversity of interpretation. Religious matters are so intimately related to the individual that even in one lifetime his interpretation and conception of what religion is may change, from one period of his life to another, depending upon his changing understanding of the value of life itself. Each religion, from the primitive form of fetishism to the modern form of monotheism, may present special features unlike that of any other, but all religions at every time and place have helped to determine man's thoughts, emotions, and behavior.

The way in which all religions resemble one another is that they include the interrelation between the human and the superhuman or the supernatural. The theologian Paul Tillich summarizes the fundamental concept of religion as "the state of being grasped by an ultimate concern, by an infinite interest, by something one takes unconditionally seriously." (*Morality and Beyond,* Harper and Row, 1963, p. 30.) The history of religion, as an activity involving an interplay between the human and the supernatural, leads us through various states of development from naturism (the worship of the objects of nature), through spiritism (the worship of ancestors), polytheism, brahmanism, neoplatonism, and

other steps to the end point in historical analysis—
monotheism. In modern times, and for the purpose of
our discussion, we may safely say that religion has
reference to man's relation to divinity and to his
obligations to his Creator. The bond uniting man to
God entails a moral obligation to render God the
reverence and obedience due to Him as the sustainer
of all life and the source of all being.

Recognition of God as an object of love and adora-
tion implies an obligation to act in accordance to the
present principles of morality discovered by our reason and our feelings. Webster defines the distinction
between religion and morality as follows: "As distinguished from *morality, religion* denotes the influences and motives of human duty which are found
in the character and will of God, while morality describes the duties of man, which true religion always
influences."

Morality Rooted in Religion

The influence of religion on the moral duties of
man finds its expression in our consciences, and we
may find the terms "conscience," "morality," and
"religion" used interchangeably. Asks the court:
"For what is religion but morality, with a sanction
drawn from a future state of rewards and punishments?" (*McAllister v. Marshall*, 6 Bin. 338, 6 Am.
Dec. 458 [Pa. 1814].) The identity of meaning given
to such terms as "religious impulse," "religious belief," "the voice of conscience," and "moral obligation" points to the close interrelationship between
morality and religion. Reason and logic without the

aid of religious belief are not adequate to relate the individual to his fellowman and to his universe.

We have remarked earlier that Kant accepted a moral universal law as pragmatically necessary. He expressed his sentiments as follows: "There are two things which, the more I contemplate them, the more they fill my mind wih admiration—the starry heavens above me and the moral law within me." In commenting on this sentiment of Kant, the prominent American jurist John Forrest Dillon wrote in his commentaries *The Laws and Jurisprudence of England and America:*

> "Not less wonderous than the revelations of the starry heavens and much more important . . . is the moral law which Kant found within himself, and which is likewise found within, and is consciously recognized by every man. This moral law holds its dominion by divine ordination over us all, from which escape or evasion is impossible. This moral law is the eternal and indestructible sense of justice and of right written by God on the living tables of the human heart and revealed in his Holy Word."

The importance of revelation within the moral law was stressed by Sir William Blackstone. The illustrious English jurist expressed in his famous *Commentaries on the Laws of England* the opinion that because of our first ancestor's transgression our reason is "corrupt" and our understanding "full of ignorance and error." This, he argues, made it necessary for Providence to reveal its laws. These precepts are revealed to us in the Holy Scriptures, which are to be a part of the original law of nature as "they tend in all their consequence to man's felicity."

What is the impact of the Judaeo-Christian tradition on the morality of our laws? The Supreme Court of Appeals of West Virginia, reviewing a case of the removal from office of a prosecuting attorney found guilty of gross immorality, analyzed the governing standards of morality and reached the conclusion that our morality is more in harmony with the Mosaic interpretation of the moral law than with the "truly divine" interpretation given to man by Christ. According to Christ's teaching, man holds his body, mind, soul, and property by divine grant in trust for the benefit of his fellowman. This teaching calls for complete devotion to the welfare of humanity and for the establishment of a kingdom of perfect righteousness. "It makes," states the court, "the laws of morality concur fully with the laws of religion. According to it, he who serves man best worships God best, and he who worships God best serves man best."

While this divine interpretation of the Commandments is intended to secure perfection, the Mosaic interpreation, states the court, is "founded on absolute justice between man and man." Every man belongs to himself, has the right to do as he pleases, so long as he does nothing to interfere with his environment and accords the same right to others. The morality of our laws, concludes the court, "is the morality of the Mosaic interpretation of the Ten Commandments, modified only as to degree or kind of punishment inflicted." (*Moore et al. v. Strickling*, 46 W. Va. 515, 33 S.E. 174 [1899].)

Some may not accept this distinction between the two interpretations of the Commandments. Spinoza, for instance, looked upon the Jewish and the Christian religions as one and made no separation betwen the Old and New Testaments. The eternal wisdom of God, he wrote, "has shown itself forth in all things, but chiefly in the mind of man, and most of all in Jesus Christ." There is no doubt that the New Testament reaffirms and emphasizes the moral standards and obligations laid down in the Ten Commandments. Furthermore, the morality of our laws is not in fact limited to the Mosaic interpretations of the Ten Commandments. In analyzing these laws, we shall also discover the great impact of Christ's teaching, to mention only the special consideration that repentance has received in our courts and the qualities of forgiveness and compassion that are bound up in our judicial system.

The concept that morality is rooted in religion goes back as far as Plato and Aristotle. Plato believed that a nation cannot be strong unless it has faith in God. According to Aristotle, God is the first cause and the final cause—the purpose—of the world. The question that remains to be answered is: Are all systems of morality rooted in religion? In reviewing the various ethical traditions, we will, of course, find that some of them are consistently atheistic or agnostic. It remains to be seen whether these ethical traditions are fully consistent with the body of laws on which our nation is based.

We find two central groups of values glorified by ethical tradition. One is distinctly religious or remains in some sort of religious context; the other is divorced from religion. To the first group belong the traditional cardinal virtues listed by our courts: justice, prudence, temperance, and fortitude. *(Lyon v. Mitchell* 36 N.Y. 235, 238 [1867].) We may add wisdom, duty, truth, love, liberty, fidelity, honesty, and other similar virtues that develop the whole man. These in their origin are related to some kind of belief in God and consequently have special meaning within the context of religious faith. "Sound morals as taught by the wise men of antiquity, as confirmed by the precepts of the gospel . . . are unchangeable. They are the same yesterday and today." *(Zorach v. Clauson,* 343, U.S. 306, 313, 72. S. Ct. 679, 684, 96 L. Ed. 954 [1952].)

In our discussion of the various concepts of conscience, we pointed out that the moralists who are known as intuitionists believe that moral ideas are innate in man, that they are the inner law of our true being, the "silent voice" of our nature as man. Among them, Immanuel Kant believed that the supreme principle which man must follow is the categorical, unconditional moral imperative. Paul Tillich considers this unconditional character as the imperative's religious quality: "[T]he religious dimension of the moral imperative is its unconditional character." *(Morality and Beyond,* p. 33.) The divinely revealed natural moral law is in full harmony with the divinely created human nature. The ultimate moral principle is love, which should not be identified with charity or pity. Love is the highest work of the divine spirit, as described in the book of I Corinthians: "[I]f I have no love, I am nothing. I may dole out all I possess, or even give my body to be

burnt, but if I have no love, I am none the better. . . .
There is nothing love cannot face; there is no limit to
its faith, its hope, and its endurance." (13:2-3, 7.)
Love, therefore, includes and even transcends all the
other virtues. In social institutions, spiritual freedom
and human brotherhood are expressions of love.

Morality Not Rooted in Religion

Among the chief "virtues" of the second group of
values—without roots in religion—we might list the
desire of pleasure and the desire of power. The intrinsic aim of man—which according to Plato is "to
become as much as possible similar to God" or as
defined by Aristotle is participation in the eternal
divine self-institution—is what gives the moral imperative its unconditional character. Such an unconditional character is lacking when man's aim is the
greatest possible amount of pleasure to be derived
from life. Contrast this view with the biblical one:
"Set your affection on things above, not on things on
the earth" (Colossians 3:2) and "It is the spirit that
gives life, the flesh has nothing to offer." (John 6:63.)
The hedonistic tradition, which extols pleasure, did
not come from the Hebrew prophets and lawgivers
and is not a part of the Judaeo-Christian morality
which is the heritage of Western nations.

The doctrine that pleasure is the highest good,
known as hedonism, has its own ancient roots. The
principle that pleasure is the supreme good and indeed the only intrinsic good with moral significance
for the individual was advocated by the Cyrenaic
doctrine formulated by Aristippus, the Greek

philosopher of Cyrene (5th-4th Century B.C.). In the dialogue *Gorgias,* Plato presents Socrates rejecting the contention that pleasure is the supreme good and showing the logical inadequacy of identifying pleasure with good.

Hedonism—which is egotistic and atheistic—is often unjustly confused with epicureanism and utilitarianism, which have different conceptions of the pleasant life than Cyrenaicism. The Roman poet and philosopher Lucretius Cavus in his *De Rerum Natura* (On the Nature of Things) follows Epicurus in granting that there is a god immortal and blessed but remote, who never intrudes in the affairs of men and who, therefore, is above dealing with rewards and punishments. This god lives, as a good epicurean should, in a garden of Epicurus in the clouds. Epicurus and his followers sought a pleasure that could lead to true happiness. Mere sensual enjoyment, he argues, brings unhappiness, "for it is not continuous drinkings and revellings, nor the satisfaction of lusts . . . which produce a pleasant life, but sober reasoning." The most important virtue, the beginning and the greatest good, is prudence, which is "a more precious thing even than philosophy," for it is not possible "to live pleasantly without living prudently and justly." In community life, the epicurean way consists of a pledge to assure mutual help among men, to restrain men from harming one another, and to save them from being harmed.

The British utilitarians Jeremy Bentham and John Stuart Mill replace the idea of pleasure with "happiness." Bentham taught that the individual's happiness depends upon the happiness of the greatest

number. Such happiness represents the ethics of enlightened self-interest, calling for the individual's
self-restraint in his search for happiness. Mill advocated the "Greatest Happiness Principle": "as rich
as possible in enjoyments, both in point of quantity
and quality." The individual's standard of conduct
should be the best interests of society, "the greatest
happiness of the greatest number." This transition
from a sole interest in one's selfish happiness to a
more general interest in that of others implies the
natural moral law with its principle of love for our
fellowman. Mill admits this principle by pointing
out: "In the golden rule of Jesus of Nazareth, we read
the complete spirit of the ethics of utility. To do as
one would be done by, and to love one's neighbor as
oneself, constitute the ideal perfection of utilitarian
morality."

Far removed from philosophies allied closely to
systems based on the moral imperatives rooted in
religion are those so-called moral systems based
solely on the prerogatives of power. When man's aim
is merely a restless desire for power, he has divorced
himself from the Judaeo-Christian tradition. The
condemnation of such a position is richly illustrated
in the Holy Scripture, to mention only Jezebel and
Haman. Those who seeking power disobey God may
expect the punishment described in Leviticus
26:19-20: "I will break the pride of your power . . .
and your strength shall be spent in vain." The writers
of the Old Testament realized that such retribution
did not always occur in this life—Job expressed his
dismay in his cry, "Why do the wicked live, reach old
age, and grow mighty in power?" They concluded

that a just God would somehow right things in the end, and goodness would prevail over naked power.

Thus the ethical position that extols power for its own sake—like the hedonistic tradition—is alien to the Hebrew prophets and lawgivers, as well as to Christ's teachings. It begins with the Sophists as portrayed in the first book of Plato's *Republic* by Glaucon and Thrasymachus, who argue that "all men believe in their hearts that injustice is far more profitable to the individual than justice" and that "the just is always a loser in comparison with the unjust." They believe that injustice applied on a large scale is particularly rewarding, since "injustice, when on a sufficient scale, has more strength and freedom and mastery than justice." From them a straight line leads to the power politics represented by Hobbes, Machiavelli, Nietzsche, and Marx.

In his uncompromising atheism and materialism, Hobbes exalts absolute monarchy. Machiavelli divorces the prince from ethical principles, recommending that he use hypocrisy, force, and fraud to gain power. The validity of law is also derived from force: "Nothing causes a prince to be so much esteemed as giving proof of prowess."

For Nietzsche, life is will to power and, therefore, it is essentially "injury, conquest of the strange and weak, suppression, severity . . . and at least, putting it mildest, exploitation." Exploitation, he believes, is a primary organic function of living, "it is a consequence of the intrinsic Will to Power, which is precisely the Will of Life." According to Machiavelli, "it is much safer to be feared than loved . . . For it may be said of men in general that they are ungrateful, voluble, dissemblers, anxious to avoid danger, and covetous of gain." Karl Marx, in order for the proletarians to seize power, calls for a merciless revolution which will bring the collapse of capitalism.

The power politics advocated by Machiavelli and Nietzsche influenced the minds of Mussolini and Hitler. The totalitarian communist countries are carrying out the gospel of Marx. The fruits of such abuses of power are only too well-known. Today we continue to witness the atrocites taking place in countries under the yoke of communist dictatorships. We find tyranny instead of democracy, injustice and slavery instead of justice, equality in general poverty instead of prosperity, nationalism and impeialism instead of peace, and hypocritical slogans to conceal the darkness of oppression.

This darkness is the effect of a desire for power combined with a dismissal of conscience; it is expressed most effectively by the title character in Shakespeare's *Richard III:*

> "Our strong arms to be our conscience, swords
> our law.
> March on, join bravely, let to't pell-mell;
> If not to heaven, then hand in hand to hell."

Shakespeare's villains, in fact, often speak doctrines derived from the teaching of Machiavelli, who was regarded as an infamous atheistic writer in Elizabethan England.

There is, indeed, something that the teachings of those who extol power as the supreme virtue have in common—they hated religion as an opiate, as an invention of the weak to limit and to deter the strong.

As Nietzsche revels in the strength of the Superman, he pours contempt on the Judaeo-Christian ethic. The "spiritual men" of Christianity, he argues, have given comfort to the sufferers, courage to the oppressed and despairing; by preserving the sick and the suffering, they have caused the European race to deteriorate. "I regard Christianity," he writes, "as the most fatal and seductive lie that has ever yet existed—as the greatest and most injurious lie. . . . I urge people to declare open war with it." Hitler and Stalin did declare war against religion and revived cruelty in a form never known before.

In our generation, we have witnessed the fall of fascism in Italy and the fall of Nazi Germany. These events give us hope in the principle that nothing established by violence and maintained by force in opposition to what is right can endure. Nor can anything which is based on a contempt for human personality and which degrades humanity endure. Power not undergrided by spiritual force must destroy itself. Only the constructive power of spiritually creative resources can isolate the destructive forces of tyranny, divert us toward positive goals of human welfare, and help to build bridges of understanding and fellowship among peoples by mastering the moral and material resources latent in this world.

The only supreme power is God. Those who have rejected His commandment of love and who have attempted to seize that power which is His alone have brought into the world as a corollary of their power unparalleled destruction of human beings, terror, slavery, and concentration camps; they have

plunged the world into wars of unprecedented fero-
ciousness. We are reminded of the warning Aristotle
issued in his *Politics:* "For man, when perfected, is
the best of the animals, but when separated from law
and justice, he is the worst of all; . . . wherefore, if he
have not virtue, he is the most unholy and the most
savage of animals." What distinguishes man from
animal is the freedom of choice between the moral
values whose roots are in religion and the values
separated from religion. This fundamental choice
can be made only by means of the profound understanding which comes from knowledge of the purpose of life.

Knowledge of Moral Principles

According to Spinoza, the endeavor to understand
"is the first and only basis of virtue," because "the
greatest good is the knowledge of the union, which
mind has with the whole nature . . . The more the
mind knows, the better it understands its forces and
the order of nature; the more it understands its forces
or strength, the better it will be able to divest itself
and lay down the rules of itself." Throughout the
great philosophical tradition which we have tried to
trace, there is the deeply rooted idea that understanding leads to right action. For Socrates, knowledge is virtue. For Plato, only knowledge produces
a harmonious man capable of governing his desires
and passions. Our forefathers declared in the Northwest Ordinance, to which I have referred previously,
that knowledge is necessary, along with religion and
morality, for good government, because the inculca-
tion of religion and morality can take place only

through the diffusion of knowledge. The kind of knowledge to which all of these referred is not mere abstract reasoning or the accumulation of facts. Knowledge, in order to explain the purposeful creation of the universe and guide our actions, must be grounded in the true values of life provided by religion and morality.

Knowledge in this deeper sense can flourish only when it is related to some kind of belief in God and immortality; by itself it cannot accomplish the aim of human life, which searches for something beyond mere survival. Without the direction of a moral code, knowledge becomes aimless and meaningless; but when supplemented by moral principles, it creates a climate in which commitment to service may emerge. Supplemented by moral principles, it shatters the illusions of those who refuse to acknowledge the dependent character of man's life and put their trust in wealth, security, pleasure, and power.

As John Wesley insisted, only the blended light of knowledge and vital piety, by controlling our violent, unsocial impulses and uncoordinated passions, can guide individuals and nations into harmony and prevent conflicts. This is the essence of the interrelation between knowledge, religion, and morality. When knowledge and religion are fused into one force—which is understanding—it is capable of grasping the highest truths: "The Lord by wisdom hath founded the earth, by understanding hath he established the heavens." (Proverbs 3:19.) It is the only force which can lift up humbled humanity and help it to fulfill God's call for a holiness of life which Wesley called "social holiness," love and service to all mankind.

Chapter II

NATURAL JUSTICE AND NATURAL RIGHTS

What Kind of Virtue?

The battle cry of the French Revolution was *Liberté, egalité, fraternité.* The maxim of the American Revolution was "Taxation without representation is tyranny." In the nineteenth century, the slogan of the Polish patriots in their struggle against Czarist Russia was "For your freedom and ours." Later this slogan was adopted by progressive democratic world leaders, who identified it with the course of liberty. In Russia itself in 1917, the Bolsheviks sought a "dictatorship of the proletariat," and their slogan sounded everywhere: "Peace to the army, land to the peasants, control of the factories to the workers."

All these rallying cries prompt us to ask why, in times of turmoil and tension, when people demand the rectification of errors and atrocities, they place the highest values on freedom, brotherhood, and equality in the distribution of wealth and of opportunity, without mentioning justice as one of the moral, spiritual, economic, or political aims to be achieved.

What kind of a virtue is justice? Epicurus finds that "justice never is anything in itself" but is "a kind of compact not to harm or be harmed" in our dealings with one another. Saint Augustine believes that we are in the midst of evils which cannot be removed from our life either by justice, prudence, or temperance, unless these virtues are used in service to God, for there is in man "a certain just order of nature, so that the soul is subjected to God, and the flesh to the soul, and consequently both soul and flesh to God ..." There is no justice nor any other true virtue, states Augustine, where there is no religion.

Aristotle in his *Nichomachean Ethics*, admitting the ambiguity of the terms "justice" and "injustice," concludes that justice is "not part of virtue but virtue entire," that it is "often thought to be the greatest of virtues," and that "neither evening nor morning star is so wonderful." It is, he believes, the complete virtue in its fullest sense, because he who possesses it can exercise his virtue not only in himself but toward his neighbor also. The importance of justice in the relationship with other persons is also stressed in Artistotle's discussion of friendship, the virtue "most indispensable for life." When people are friends, he writes, "they have no need of justice, but when they are just, they need friendship in addition. In fact, the just in the fullest sense is regarded as constituting an element of friendship."

To Plato a just society is a perfect society. As the effective "harmony of the whole," justice is the supreme, overarching virtue. It does not permit the several elements within man "to interfere with one another." Justice binds the three principles involved in moral behavior. These principles or basic elements, according to Plato, are: (1) wisdom, which governs the soul by reason; (2) temperance, which calls for the rational regulation of our desires or appetites; and (3) courage, the spirit which retains and enforces "the commands of reason" about what we ought or ought not to do.

The harmony of these three faculties constitutes justice. When this harmonious condition is achieved, the just man "sets in order his own inner life, and is his own master and his own law, and at peace with himself." When strife arises among the three principles, injustice occurs—the "rising up of a part of the soul against the whole," creating confusion and disease, which destroy the natural order of the personality. Justice, states Plato, is an institution of natural order, and injustice creates things "at variance with the natural order."

In the Old and New Testaments, justice is identified with the very essence of divinity. The invocation of divine justice signifies not a request to satisfy a claim but a request for grace: "Hear my prayer, O Lord, give ear to my supplications: in thy faithfulness answer me, and in thy righteousness." (Psalm 143:1.) Moses describes the Lord as "a God of truth and without iniquity, just and right is He." (Deuteronomy 32:4.) As St. Thomas expressed it: *cum ipse sit jus justicia* ("The justice of God is inherent in Himself"). There is, therefore, a distinction between divine justice and human justice. Divine justice, of a metaphysical character, represents God's will, in which justice—which comprises the gift of grace—is fused with pity, goodness, and wisdom. Human justice calls for conformity to the divine will. In the words of the Gospel, "Blessed are they which do hunger and thirst after righteousness; for they shall be filled." (Matthew 5:6.)

A Word of Many Meanings

The definitions of justice are so various that it is unsatisfactory to single out one. The meaning of the word cannot be defined with precision. It is sufficient to say that the end of justice is to protect our natural and civil rights in our relations to other individuals, to our society, and to the state. Justice rectifies the errors we commit when we transgress the allowed limits of our natural rights, or violate man-made laws, or exercise the powers of government arbitrarily. Because of the restraint imposed by natural justice upon the various natural inalienable rights, we have to acknowledge the primacy of justice as the supreme value.

Discussion of the various kinds of justice reveals conflict and confusion, because justice is a word of many meanings. Among the numerous definitions of distinct kinds of justice, we shall list some of the more important ones. Aristotle originated the distinction between distributive and commutative (rectificatory) justice. The first one governs the distribution of rewards and punishments to each according to his merits and services. Since it does not consider all men equal, distributive justice discriminates between them by observing a just proportion and comparison so that neither equal persons have unequal things nor unequal persons equal things. Commutative justice governs contracts and is based on equality between the parties. Its object is to render to everyone what belongs to him without regard to his personal worth or merits, so that no one gains by another's loss.

Pufendorf—the German jurist, statesman, and historian (1632-1694)—divides justice into imperfect or universal and perfect or particular. The first discharges duties that cannot be exacted by the law; the latter deals with duties strictly demanded by law. The French jurist Toullier (1752-1835) prefers the division of internal and external justice as the only division "clear, exact, and useful" (*La division de la justice en intérieure ou extérieure nous parait la seule claire, la seule exacte, la seule utile*). Internal justice, he states, conforms to our will and is the object of morality; external deals with our actions and is the object of jurisprudence. The medieval French jurist A. Michel held the opinion that all kinds of justice—whether distributive, commutative, or legal—are social justice, since they concern the relation between man and man.

The list of suggested divisions of justice could be continued, but it seems that we have reached the point of realization that we must use the term "justice" carefully and limit our discussion to only one of its aspects. For this reason, our comments will be devoted to the idea of natural justice and one of its great purposes—the preservation of natural, fundamental rights, which should be sacred.

Natural justice, according to our courts, is founded "in equity, in honesty and right." It dictates that we should do what is "fair." That which is fair, the courts have stated, "is a question of standards of conduct, about which men may differ." Natural justice, like natural law, is revealed to us by the light of reason and remains in essential agreement with the constitution of human nature. According to some

philosophers, it is the judgment based on the eternal
rule of righteousness which God inscribed upon the
heart of every man, which enables us to know truth
from falsehood and good from evil. President Calvin
Coolidge referred to that eternal character of law
when he announced that "men do not make laws,
they do but discover them."

When we accept the premise of the existence of an
ethical imperative, we have to answer the question
whether there exists an interdependence of law, justice, and morals. For Calvin, the moral law "prescribed to men of all ages and natures" is identical
with a declaration of natural law. "This equity," he
wrote, "must alone be the scope, and rule, and end,
of all laws." Thomas Aquinas argued that "tyrannical
law, not being according to reason, is not law at all in
the true and strict sense but is a perversion of law."
Saint Augustine offers the far-reaching conclusion
that "that which is not just seems to be no law at all."
Martin Luther rejected the whole body of canon law,
which governed the medieval church and by which
the church sought to govern society in general. In
December of the year 1520, he staged a bookburning
on the bank of the Elbe; into the flames went the
whole library of canon law, which, according to
Luther, "has arisen in the devil's name."

Equity Law

Equity law owes its existence to this same sense of
discrepancy between the law as it exists and the law
as it ought to be. It arose from the defectiveness of
human laws and their inability to remedy their own

deficiencies or to moderate their harshness when applied to a particular case. Grotius defined equity as *Correctrix eius in quo lex propter universalitatem deficit* ("the correction of that in which the law is lacking because of its very universality"). The principle of equity was known as early as the Roman period. The Roman praetors held the first courts of equity, and the *jus praetorium* was a collection of rules introduced by the praetors to protect the citizens from the iniquitous operation of municipal law.

From Rome this practice was transplanted to almost every civilized nation. In some countries the king, in others a special counsel, reviewed the decisions of the courts when a party could not obtain justice through ordinary channels or sought moderation of the rigors of the law when applied to an individual case. With the growth of civilization and the extension of commerce, the equity courts accommodated their jurisdiction to these growing exigencies, thus gaining strength as time went on. When the existing law did not respond to changes and its settled principles operated inadequately, the natural result was a search for new avenues to express the moral element which permeates the judicial process.

There is no agreement among the American legal giants, or at least there is uncertainty on the part of the Supreme Court, as to whether law and morals are separate modes of social control or whether they are to be made identical by conforming the existing legal precepts to the requirements of a reasoned system of morals. Justice Benjamin Cardozo in his *Paradoxes of Legal Science* stressed the need for a judge to

respond to a "moral urge" and claimed that as a result
of such a response "the moral norm and the jural
have been brought together, and are one."
Whenever a conflict exists, Cardozo held, "moral
values are to be preferred to economic, and
economic to aesthetic." (Columbia University Press,
1928, pp. 46, 57.)

While the British Chief Justice Lord Mansfield
elaborated extensively on the need to inject moral
concepts into the law, another illustrious legal re-
former, Jeremy Bentham, believed that such concepts as natural rights and natural justice prove "two
things only, the heat of passion, and the darkness of
understanding." He asserted that the only test of the
goodness or badness of a law is its actual effect on
human beings, their pain, and their pleasure.

In Germany, Friedrich Karl von Savigny (1779-
1861), one of the foremost jurists of his age, was one
of the earliest adherents of the historical school of
jurisprudence. He resisted the imposition of legal
codes and denied the efficacy of legal reform alien to
the people it has to serve. What binds people, states
Savigny, "is the common conviction of the people,
the kindred consciousness of an inward necessity,
*excluding all notion of an accidental and arbitrary
origin.* [Emphasis added.]" In other words, Savigny
saw in historic experience a substitute for the standard of reason, with no need of conformity to an *a
priori* principle of right or just law such as that offered by the doctrine of natural law and justice.

The essence of Savigny's idea was expressed by
Justice Oliver Wendell Holmes when he wrote in his
The Common Law:

"The life of the law has not been logic: it has been experience. The felt necessities of the time, the prevalent moral and political theories, intuitions of public policy, avowed or unconscious, even the prejudices which judges share with their fellow-men have had a good deal more to do than the syllogism in determining the rules by which men should be governed."

In the United States, Justices Holmes and Felix Frankfurter were among the most illustrious and outspoken jurists who believed that moral and ethical values should not be injected into the law. They opposed any attempt on the part of judges to make the law conform to an ideal moral standard. Justice Frankfurter, dissenting in the case of *West Virginia Board of Education v. Barnette,* wrote that it can never be emphasized too much "that one's opinion about the wisdom or evil of a law should be excluded altogether when one is doing one's duty on the bench." (319 U.S. 624, 647, 63 S. Ct. 1178, 1189 [1943].)

Justice Holmes, skeptical as to our knowledge "of the goodness or badness of laws," held that a judge's responsibility is to enforce in good faith and to the best of his ability "whatever constitutional laws Congress or anybody sees fit to pass." His decisions, for instance, enforced antitrust laws, although as a believer in the theory of the survival of the strong he viewed the Sherman Act as one based on economic incompetence and ignorance. As reported by Francis Biddle, a former Attorney General of the United States, Justice Holmes exclaimed in a conversation with John Davis, the Solicitor General of the United States, after trying an antitrust case: "Of course I know, and every other sensible man knows, that the Sherman law is damned nonsense, but if my country wants to go to hell, I am here to help it." *(Justice Holmes, Natural Law, and the Supreme Court,* The Macmillan Company, 1961, p. 9.) He believed that "law, being a practical thing, must found itself on actual forces."

Holmes rejected the concept of abstract justice when he wrote "that the Common Law is not a brooding omnipresence in the sky and the U.S. is not subject to some mystic overlaw that it is bound to obey." The difference between abstract justice and the law was also described in forceful terms by Justice Oran M. Roberts of the Supreme Court of Texas, one of the greatest judges the state has ever had. (He was also Governor of Texas at the time The University of Texas was established.) He defines justice as "a dictate of right, according to the common consent of mankind generally or of that portion of mankind who may be governed by the same principles and morals." It represents, he believes, "a chaotic mass of principles," while law classifies and reduces to order the same mass of principles and puts them in the shape of rules agreed upon by common consent.

Justice, states Roberts, "is the virgin gold of the mines, that passes for its intrinsic worth in every case, but is subject to varying value, according to the scales through which it passes. Law is the coin from the mint, with its value ascertained and fixed, with the stamp of government upon it which assures and denotes its value." Concludes Justice Roberts, "To follow the dictates of justice, when in harmony with the law, must be a pleasure; but to follow the rules of law, in their true spirit, to whatever consequences they may lead, is a duty."

Courts and Legislatures

Judges are not at liberty to substitute their own ideas for the wishes of legislators. They cannot substitute their social, political, and economic beliefs for the judgment of legislative bodies, which are elected to pass laws. "It must be remembered that legislatures are ultimate guardians of the liberties and welfare of the people in quite as great degree as courts." (*Missouri, K & T Co. v. May,* 194 U.S. 267, 270, 24 S. Ct. 638, 639 [1904].)

Justice in the judicial sense calls for exact conformity to obligatory law. Judicial power can be exercised only for the purpose of giving effect to the will of the law and not to the will of the judge. Judicial discretion is a legal discretion to be exercised according to known and established rules, not an arbitrary power of the judge. The English statesman and philosopher Francis Bacon wrote in 1625: "Judges ought to remember that their office is to interpret law and not to make or give law." Montesquieu believed that "the judges of the nation are only the mouths that pronounce the words of the law, inanimate beings, who can moderate neither its force nor its rigor." Chief Justice Marshall stressed that "judicial power is never exercised for the purpose of giving effect to the will of the judge; always for the purpose of giving effect to the will of the legislature; or in other words, to the will of the law." *(Osborn v. Bank of the United States,* 9 Wheat. 738, 866 [1824].) History gives ample evidence that mankind benefits more from an administration of justice where rights are determined by a system of rules rather than by a sense of abstract justice as conceived by the judge.

To follow the rules of law is the duty of the court, which is a mere instrument of the law. This does not imply that law always fulfills our notions of the dictates of justice. There are moral claims and duties, comprehended under humanity, benevolence, or charity, which law does not enforce; their fulfillment is left to man's conscience and honor. Law is not always accepted as moral by an enlightened public opinion nor does it always punish or restrain some of the violations of our moral sense.

The history of jurisprudence gives ample evidence that law cannot be separated from moral values. There are numerous reasons why moral concern is interwoven in the exercise of judicial justice. The nature of the judicial process, as projected by President Theodore Roosevelt in his message to the Congress of the United States of December 8, 1908, met with severe criticism on the part of those who believed that the only authority of a judge is to follow the rule of law. In that message President Roosevelt declared:

> "The chief lawmakers in our country may be, and often are, the judges, because they are the final seal of authority. Every time they interpret contract, property, vested rights, due process of law, liberty, they necessarily enact into law parts of a

system of social philosophy; and such interpretation is fundamental, they give direction to all lawmaking. The decisions of the courts on economic and social questions depend upon their economic and social philosophy; and for the peaceful progress of our people during the twentieth century we shall owe most to those judges who hold to a twentieth century economic and social philosophy and not to a long outgrown philosophy, which was itself the product of primitive economic conditions."

Changing Views

The changes that constantly occur in our dynamic society—economic, social, and political—create new demands which have an impact on the courts' reasoning. Because of these demands, the principle of adhering to precedent—which offers continuity with the past and attempts to guarantee that all people will be treated alike—no longer satisfies our society's expectation that the judicial process can be adapted to varying conditions. The Supreme Court of the United States has explicitly asserted its right to overrule a prior constitutional decision when it realizes that the prior principle is wrong. The Court has stated that it feels justified in having more freedom to overrule prior constitutional decisions than to change its interpretations of other laws, since the Constitution is difficult to amend, while mere statutes or other legal principles which do not raise constitutional issues can easily be changed by legislative action. (*Smith v. Allwright,* 321 U.S. 649, 665 [1944].)

With respect to segregated schools, for instance, the courts adhered for over half a century to the doctrine of "separate but equal" that appeared in 1896 in the United States Supreme Court ruling on the case of *Plessy v. Ferguson*. (163 U.S. 537 [1896].) Under that doctrine, equality of treatment is accorded when the races are provided substantially equal facilities, even though these facilities be separate. Over fifty years later, in 1954 in the case of *Brown v. Board of Education of Topeka*, the Supreme Court held that segregation of children in public schools solely on the basis of race, even though the physical facilities and other tangible factors may be equal, deprives the children of the minority group of equal educational opportunities in contravention of the Equal Protection Clause of the Fourteenth Amendment. The Court concluded that in the field of public education the doctrine of "separate but equal" has no place, because "we cannot turn the clock . . . to 1896 when *Plessy v. Ferguson* was written. We must consider public education in the light of its full development and its present place in American life throughout the Nation." (347 U.S. 492 [1954].) Decisions are reversed as our perception of justice and natural rights develop.

Court decisions around the turn of this century, which declared as unconstitutional a legislative act making it unlawful for an employer to prohibit an employee from joining, or to require him to withdraw from, a trade or labor union or any other lawful organization can hardly serve as precedents in cases in the field of labor law as it exists today, in the wake of the New Deal, the Fair Deal, and the Great Society. Our courts find fewer and fewer occasions to invoke as precedents decisions issued before state welfare became a way of life in the United States. New restraints imposed by labor and civil rights legislation, by the Fair Housing and Equal Employment Opportunity acts, by Affirmative Action and environmental regulation have changed the concepts of "property," "free enterprise," and "liberty" embodied in our laws. The almost unrestrained enjoyment of the use of property and of economic liberty which once characterized our system has disappeared. These changes have both influenced and been influenced by our judicial system.

Court decisions which, after they have been duly tested by experience, are found inconsistent with new conditions or with social welfare are destined for abandonment. Prominent French jurists advocate the judicial interpretation of statutes in *"le sense évolutif"* that calls for inquiring what the legislator would have willed if he had known what the new conditions would be. In the endless process of testing and retesting the structure and desires of our society, precedents must be discarded or modified when they become inconsistent with new rules of conduct and changes in the fundamental desires of the society. As the late Justice William O. Douglas pointed out, the use of precedents or the principle of *stare decisis* "must give way before the dynamic component of history." ("Stare Decisis," 49 *Columbia Law Review* 735, 737 [1949].) To paraphrase this statement, we may say that precedents must give way before the compelling force of natural justice and of moral and ethical principles that move forward under the dynamics of human history.

Morals and the Law

The tradition of natural law has a claim on the administration of justice. In my book *The Third Way* (The University of Texas at Dallas, 1980, pp. 155-175), I defended the position that the moral values that underlay the founding of this country can be found in the tradition of natural law. Our basic assertion was and is that the natural law is revealed to mankind for the conservation of man's nature and the promotion of his purpose of existence and well-being. We do not propose to discuss again the merits of this assertion or of the different schools of natural law, but we do wish to dispute the position of those who reject the concept of eternal order by discarding all absolutes, including natural law. The advocates of divorcing the ethical order from the legal admit only the existence of a relationship between morals and the law, not their interdependence. As Holmes expressed it, "The law is the witness and the external deposit of our moral life. The history is the history of the moral development of the race."

There undoubtedly exists "a relationship" between Nazi or Soviet laws and the morality of Hitler, Stalin, and their vicious henchmen. The Nazi and Soviet systems of justice which resulted from such a relationship are fearful examples of the perversion of justice when divorced from the traditional concept of morality. Is it the role of justice to enforce laws which are the "deposit" of a "morality" designed to trample on human lives and rights? No more than other men can judges ignore Edmund Burke's warning, "All that is necessary for the forces of evil to win this world is for good men to do nothing." The courts of

Nazi Germany and of Soviet Russia became agencies subservient to the dictates of the parties in power, carrying out the instructions received from party bosses. The effects are well-known.

The fight against arbitrary tyranny, cynicism, and dictatorship, states Paul Tillich, "can be won only by a new foundation of natural law and justice." (*Love, Power, and Justice*, Oxford University Press, 1954, p. 56.) No one questions the existence of a relationship between "law and the moral development of the race," but it is their interdependence which causes the performance of one's legal duty to include obedience to the urges of morality, revealed to us by the Author of Nature through the force of reason. Such a morality resting on the foundation of a belief in and reverence for the Creator and on obedience to His will enables man to know truth from falsehood, freedom from slavery, and good from evil.

Justice calls for putting into effect the will of the law, but because of the interdependence between moral concern and the exercise of judicial justice, a judge should keep in mind the Psalmist's advice: "Thou hast commanded us to keep thy precepts diligently. O that my ways were directed to keep thy statutes! Then shall I not be ashamed when I have respect unto all thy commandments." (Psalm 119: 4-6.) There no doubt comes a time, wrote Judge Learned Hand, "when a statute is so obviously oppressive and absurd that it can have no justification in any sane polity."

Sir William Blackstone, the English legal commentator who had an immense influence on American jurisprudence, wrote:

"This law of nature being co-eval with mankind
and dictated by God himself, is of course superior
in obligation to any other. It is binding over all the
globe, in all countries, and at all times; no human
laws are of any validity, in contrary to this; and
such of them as are valid derive all their force, and
all their authority mediately or immediately, from
the original."

To this powerful statement the famous commentator
adds that, in order to apply this law to exigencies that
may arise in particular cases, we have to discover
"what the law of nature directs in every cir-
cumstance of life."

Moral values are more flexible than legal rules in
meeting the dictates of natural justice, which responds to the demands of changing "circumstances
of life" and new values. Natural justice is universal
in its essence and may vary in its applications to
particular circumstances. Law is a generative
mechanism sharing with Nature the capacity for
growth and adaptation. When new conditions arise,
old principles may be broadened or adapted to ac-
commodate new insights.

A legislative body is not omnipotent. An act of the
legislature contrary to the principles of the Constitution cannot be considered a rightful exercise of legislative authority. It has been repeatedly held that the
exercise of police power by a state or municipality
gives it authority to enact laws or ordinances which
pertain to public safety, public health, or public morals. Since it is a judicial question whether a legislature has transcended the limit of this authority, it is

the duty of the courts to look at the substance of legislative action in the field of public safety, health, or morals, subject to constitutional limitations or restraint. In the absence of concrete pronouncements concerning public morals, a judge, as Cardozo expressed it, has to "look into himself," and the moral element enters into his reasoning.

The same free judicial movement takes place when a statute uses representative terms. For instance, in interpreting the constitutional rights of life, liberty, and property—which we shall discuss later—the courts have taken the position that the terms "life," "liberty," and "property" are representative terms and "cover every right to which a member of the body politic is entitled under the law." Their comprehensive scope, according to the courts' interpretation, embraces the rights of self-defense, freedom of speech, religious and political freedom, exemption from arbitrary arrests—"all our liberties, personal, civil, and political—in short, all that makes life worth living." What makes life worth living? The judge must find the answer by looking "into himself" and by searching for the general moral rules which govern society.

As we have mentioned, a number of judges who have written illustrious chapters in the history of our jurisprudence have advocated judicial objectivity as the primary responsibility of the courts. Adhering to the principle *dura lex sed lex* ("Hard law, but the law"), they have advocated the severest intellectual detachment from one's own opinion and the enforcement of laws and contracts in accordance with the evidence and recognized principles of law.

Judges, however, do not live in a vacuum. Reviewing a case in which the government refused to make payment to a steel company which had made abnormal profits (22 percent) from the production of ships during World War I, the Supreme Court took the position that the government should be held to the contract unless there were valid and appropriate reasons known to the law for relieving it from its obligations. But Justice Frankfurter, who as we have indicated was one of the most outspoken advocates of judical objectivity and of "the most alert self-restraint," wrote in his dissenting opinion: "[T]he function of the judiciary is not so limited that it must sanction the use of the federal courts as instruments of injustice in disregard of moral and equitable principles which have been a part of the law for centuries." (*United States v. Bethlehem Steel Corp.*, 315 U.S. 289, 62 S. Ct. 581 [1942].) Standards of judgment should not be subjective, but since judges are human they cannot escape the need to apply standards of natural justice.

Natural Rights

The concept of natural justice safeguards that of human rights. In one of the earliest judicial decisions elaborating on the idea of natural rights, the court stated, "Due process requires that a person be not deprived of life, liberty, or property without an opportunity to be heard in defense of his right. *This rule is founded on principles of natural justice.* [Emphasis added.]" (*Stuart v. Palmer*, 74 N.Y. 183, 30 Am. Rep. 289 [1878].) Natural rights are those which grow out of the nature of man and depend upon his personality. They are distinguished from those which are created by positive laws enacted by a duly constituted government necessary to maintain an orderly organized society.

To discuss the discrepancy assumed by some philosophers between the doctrines of natural law *(lex naturalis)* and natural right *(ius naturae)* over against the individualistic doctrine of natural rights is to prolong an old and often confusing controversy. The meaning of the term "Law of Nature" as used by John Locke is substantially the same as that of "natural right" and "natural rights." Locke greatly influenced Jefferson, and the infusion of the idea of natural rights with the spirit of natural law found its expression in our Declaration of Independence. Locke and Jefferson believed that "man, being the workmanship of one omnipotent and infinitely wise Maker," has rights on his own to freedom, food, shelter, and security—to the satisfaction of fundamental needs. Unless these rights are realized, human life is frustrated, if not impossible.

These natural rights remain constant anytime and anywhere. The Greek Princess Antigone, in Sophocles' drama of the same name, invokes

> "The unwritten laws of God that know not change.
> They are not of today nor yesterday,
> But live forever, nor can man assign
> When first they sprang to being."

Thus she defended her disobedience of the tyrant

Creon's decree forbidding her to bury her brother Polyneices' body.

For Cicero the natural law emanates from divine reason "implanted in nature," and natural rights are given by God to man for the promotion of his well-being. According to Grotius and Pufendorf, there is a divinely-originated, universal need for community, and because of man's involvement in the life of society, human rights preserve the community and when enforced sufficiently make life in society tolerable.

According to Locke, men were endowed with certain natural rights before there was a state. Marx, Engels, and Lenin reject his concept of natural law and natural rights. Lenin argued that "law and state are not two distinct phenomena . . . but are two sides of the same phenomenon: class dominance." For Marx a society based on law is a "juridical fiction." Legal relations could not "be explained by the so-called general process of the human mind, but they are rooted in the material conditions of life." Engels wrote that legal principles are "only economic reflexes."

Rejecting the existence of eternal principles, Marx rejected also the existence of natural rights. Since he located the sources of law in the force of production, according to him the material order has priority over the spiritual order. Law, justice, and morality are a superstructure, while economic conditions are the substructure or the foundation of society. Consequently, man is only an economic tool in the hand of the police state. Such neglect of natural human rights brings only tyranny and slavery. The ramifications of such neglect are endless. While our courts,

for instance, have stated that "the right of privacy—
having its origin in natural law—is immutable and
absolute, and transcends the power of any authority
to change or abolish it" (*McGovern v. Van Riper*, 137
N.J. Eq. 24, 33, 43 A.2d 514, 519 [1945]), in the
omnipotent communist state there is no place for
privacy or solitude—unless in a prison cell.

The American conception of natural fundamental
rights, which should be beyond the reach of any
government, is broader than the protection offered to
the English by the Magna Charta, which protects
rights only against the monarch. The Magna Charta
took the form of prohibitions limiting the power of
the King rather than a list of rights such as those
embodied in the Constitution of the United States.
The Declaration of Independence and Amendments
to the Constitution protect these "inalienable
rights," based on truths which are "self-evident,"
against both the executive and legislative branches
of government. The independent judiciary, headed
by the United States Supreme Court, has the power
to declare the acts of the other two branches of government unconstitutional, thus offering an "impenetrable bulwark" against any attempt to violate
the natural rights embodied in the Constitution.

Such an "impenetrable bulwark" was envisioned
by James Madison when he proposed in the Bill of
Rights: "[I]ndependent tribunals of justice will consider themselves in a peculiar manner the guardian
of these rights; they will be an impenetrable bulwark
against every assumption of power in the legislative
or executive." These natural rights include the right
to personal liberty, to individual property, to the

worship of God according to the dictates of one's own conscience, to equal protection of the laws and to due process of law, to immunity from unreasonable searches and from cruel punishment, and to such other protections as are indispensable to preserve and favor the dignity of man. Because of the most comprehensive scope of human rights, we shall limit our discussion to the so-called trinity of rights, for which—according to our Declaration of Independence—governments among men are instituted: the security of life, liberty, and property guaranteed by the Fifth and Fourteenth Amendments.

The fundamental maxims of a free government require that the established individual rights should be sacred; no government is free to assume the power to violate and disregard them. The first official action of this nation reaffirmed these established principles of private rights by declaring the foundation of government in the following words: "We hold these truths to be self-evident; that all men are created equal, that they are endowed by their Creator with certain inalienable rights; that among these are life, liberty and the pursuit of happiness." These inalienable rights are beyond the control of the state.

The Constitution of the United States should always be read in the thought and spirit of the Declaration of Independence, which was intended to protect persons against the exercise of arbitrary and capricious power by any of the agencies of the federal or state government. A government that avoids interference with these rights held dear by the members

of a free society is the only dignified government of
men who are conscious of their rights and of the
destiny of humanity.

The rights a citizen has to life, liberty, and property are under the protection of the general rules that
govern a free society, and no act of legislation can
deprive a citizen of these rights. Legislators are
sworn to support the Constitution and estopped to
deny the existence of the natural rights there asserted. The Constitution grants a restrictive legislative power, within which the legislators must limit
their actions for the public welfare, and whose barriers they cannot transcend under the guise of seeking the advance of the welfare of the people. The
legislature is not omnipotent, and a law which it may
pass to take away life, liberty, or property without a
preexisting cause will be an attempt to deprive the
citizen of his constitutional rights. The constitutional
guaranty nullifies such arbitrary legislation. Legislative judgment or will is not equivalent to the "law of
the land."

Trinity of Rights

(1) Liberty and Equality

The Justinian Codification of Roman Law defined
justice as "the constant and perpetual disposition to
render every man his due." In that comprehensive
term "justice" are included the three indispensable
rights: the security of life, liberty, and property.
These three rights are grouped together and constitute a trinity of rights that are guaranteed against
unlawful deprivation by an arbitrary power. Every

departure from the safeguards provided by this trinity of rights is apt to be an appropriation of some phase of the totalitarian way.

The full scope of the liberty guaranteed by the Constitution cannot be found in or limited by the precise terms of the specific guarantees provided elsewhere in the Constitution. This liberty, wrote Justice Harlan,

> "is not a series of isolated points pricked out in terms of the taking of property; the freedom of speech, press, and religion; the right to keep and bear arms; the freedom from unreasonable searches and seizures; and so on. It is a rational continuum which, broadly speaking, includes a freedom from all substantial arbitrary impositions and purposeless restraints ... and which also recognizes, what a reasonable and sensitive judgment must, that certain interests require particularly careful scrutiny of the state needs asserted to justify their abridgment." (*Poe v. Ullman*, 367 U.S. 497, 543, 81 S. Ct. 1752, 1776, 6 L. Ed. 2d 989 [1961].)

The term "liberty" is deemed to embrace the right of man to be free in the enjoyment of the faculties with which he has been endowed by his Creator, subject only to such restraints as are necessary for the common welfare. "Liberty," as used in the federal and state constitutions, in a negative sense means freedom from restraint; in a positive sense, it means the freedom obtained by the imposition of restraint needed to promote the greatest possible amount of liberty for each. In other words, "liberty" is freedom from all restraints except such as are justly imposed by law. The interest of society calls for the absence of arbitrary restraint and not for immunity from reasonable regulations.

By the imposition upon particular persons of restraints which are deemed necessary for the general welfare, individuals give up some natural rights in consideration of equal protection and opportunity. The Bill of Rights does not license any individual to defy or ignore the correlative rights of other individuals or of society. So far as it is noticed by government, explained the court, liberty is restraint rather than license. "It is yielding of the individual will to that of many, subject to such constitutional guarantees or limitations as will preserve those rights and privileges which are admitted of all men to be fundamental."*(Weber v. Doust,* 84 Wash. 330, 146 P. 623, 625 [1915].)

Every citizen is allowed so much liberty as may exist without impairment of the *equal* rights of his fellows. Equality is an attribute of liberty. The Fourteenth Amendment intended not only that there should be no arbitrary deprivation of life, liberty, or property, but also that equal protection and security should be given to all under like circumstances in the enjoyment of their personal and civil rights. We stress the reference to "like circumstances." The "equal protection" clause of the Fourteenth Amendment means that equality is obtained if the citizen's civil rights are secured to him in the same manner and to the same extent as the same rights are accorded to all other persons under "similar circumstances."

Equality is not unlimited and cannot be maximized at the expense of liberty. It should be remembered that men are not born with equal powers and faculties; they should be offered all opportunities to develop their talents, and their creative abilities should have full opportunity of expression. Egalitarianism, which calls for the achievement of equality of conditions, leads to mediocrity and the deprivation of the citizen of his individual liberty, especially of his freedom of enterprise exercised under the principle of equality of opportunity.

All citizens are born to equal opportunities, equal political and civil rights. All citizens have equal access to the courts for the equal protection of their persons and liberties. The equal protection of laws is a pledge of the protection of equal laws. When the Assembly of the Province of Pennsylvania in 1751 ordered a bell to commemorate the fifteeth anniversary of William Penn's Charter of Privileges, which ensured freedom for all citizens of the province, it decided to inscribe on the bell's shoulder the biblical phrase: "Proclaim liberty throughout *all* the land unto *all* the inhabitants thereof." (Leviticus 25:10.)

(2) *Right to Life and Privacy*

The term "life" as employed in the Fifth and Fourteenth Amendments is a representative term. It means something more than mere animal existence. Life is a right inherent by nature in every individual which prohibits not only the mutilation of the body or destruction of any of its organs, but also prohibits the deprivation of whatever God has given to everyone with life for its enjoyment and growth. As a member of organized society, the individual surrenders to society many rights and privileges which he would be free to exercise in a state of nature, but he is not presumed to surrender rights recognized as personal, absolute, and inalienable. Among these rights is that of personal privacy.

The right of privacy, as our courts have explained, has its foundations in the instincts of nature. "It is recognized intuitively, consciousness being the witness to prove its existence." (*Bednarik v. Bednarik,* 16 A.2d 80, 18 N.J. Misc. 6331 [1940].) Derived from natural law, the concept of the right of privacy was developed under the Roman law and became incorporated into our common law. The person's right "to be let alone" is the foundation of the common law maxim, which is more than an epigram, that "every man's house is his castle," and of the law concerning unreasonable searches and seizures. The right of every person to be free from the scrutiny of others with respect to his private affairs was invoked in the most sensitive and emotional issue of abortion.

The Supreme Court in its opinion, delivered in 1973, held that the constitutional right of privacy encompasses woman's decision whether or not to terminate her pregnancy in the first trimester of pregnancy, so long as she can find a physician willing to administer an abortion. (*Roe v. Wade,* 410 U.S. 113 [1973].) The right to terminate pregnancy is, therefore, not absolute and is subject to limitations. The State does have an important, constitutionally justifiable interest in preserving and protecting the health of the pregnant woman as well as the potentiality of human life.

With respect to the health of the mother, the Court concluded that the "compelling" point is at approximately the end of the first trimester. The conclusion is based on the fact that until the end of the first trimester mortality in abortion may be less than mortality in normal childbirth. The State retains a definite interest in protecting the mother's health when an abortion is considered at a later stage of pregnancy. Therefore, after the first trimester the State may, if it chooses, regulate the abortion procedure. As to the fetus, the "compelling" point is at viability, that is, when the fetus is potentially able to live outside the mother's womb, although aided by artificial means.

The *Roe v. Wade* decision inspired a raging dispute. It became an issue in the 1980 presidential campaign and continues to be a subject of a heated controversy in the Congress. Deep convictions are behind the vigorous opposing views. One point of view asserts that one has an unlimited right to do with one's body as one pleases. Those who challenge state abortion laws point out that, when most abortion laws were first enacted, the abortion procedure was a hazardous one and that the State's interest focussed on protecting the woman's health rather than in preserving the embryo and fetus. Because medical advances have lessened this concern, at least with respect to abortion in early pregnancy, such abortion laws can thus no longer be justified by any State interest.

The other point of view argues that life begins at conception and is present throughout pregnancy, and that therefore the State has a compelling interest in protecting life from and after conception. This interest goes beyond the protection of the pregnant woman alone; the State's interest and general obligation extends to prenatal life. Since human life, as protected under the Constitution, begins with the conception, abortion would be murder.

In reaching the *Roe v. Wade* decision, the Supreme Court did not find the need to resolve the difficult question of when life begins. "When those," wrote the Court, "trained in the respective disciplines of medicine, philosophy, and theology are unable to arrive at any consensus, the judiciary, at this point in the development of man's knowledge, is not in a position to speculate as to the answer."

It is difficult "to speculate as to the answer" when attitudes toward the discussed question represent a wide divergence of not always consistent thinking. For instance, the present official belief of the Catholic Church calls for recognition of the existence of life from the moment of conception. In 1869 Pope Pius IX decreed that the soul enters the egg at conception. Yet until the nineteenth century the Aristotelian theory of "mediate animation" served as the official Roman Catholic dogma. The fetus became "animated" when it was infused with a soul. Christian theology and canon law determined the point of animation of forty days for a male and eighty days for a female. Accordingly, St. Augustine made a distinction between *embryo inanimatus* ("not yet endowed with a soul") and *embryo animatus*.

Thomas Aquinas defined movement as one of the first principles of life. The thirteenth-century English judge and writer Henry de Bracton (like most of the lawyers of his time, a priest) focussed on the quickening of the fetus as the critical point, and abortion of the quickened fetus was, in his opinion, homicide. Blackstone believed that life is the immediate gift of God and begins, in contemplation of law, as soon as an infant is able to stir in the mother's womb.

One's personal experiences, religious training, attitudes toward the family, and established moral standards will influence his conclusions whether to follow the opinion that the embryo is just a portion of the mother—not a moral or personal being—or to accept the belief so explicitly expressed by the German theologian Dietrich Bonhoeffer that "God certainly intended to create a human being" in the fetus and that by abortion "this nascent human being has been deliberately deprived of his life and that is nothing but murder."

The abortion controversy will remain highly sensitive and emotional. A statement free of emotion and of predilection can be made that the vigorous dispute on this matter demonstrates the importance of the natural right to life. It exists inherently in every man by endowment of the Creator. This right, which appertains originally and essentially to man, was wisely reaffirmed in the Constitution.

(3) Right to Property: Police Power and Eminent Domain

The third absolute right inherent in every man is the right to property, which provides all persons with equal protection and security in the free acquisition, use, enjoyment, and disposal of property. David Hume (1711-1776), the Scottish historian and philosopher whose *Treatise of Human Nature* greatly influenced our federal and state constitutions, considered that the peace and security of human society depend upon three fundamental laws: stability of possession, its transference by consent, and the performance of promises.

On a similar note the prominent American jurist, James Kent (1763-1847), who served as Chancellor of the Court of Chancery in New York and upon his retirement from the court as a professor at Columbia University, stressed the importance of the right to property when he wrote:

> "The sense of property is graciously bestowed on mankind for the purpose of rousing them from sloth and stimulating them to action, and as long as the right of acquisition is exercised in conformity to the social relations, and the moral obligations which spring from them, it ought to be sacredly protected. The natural and active sense of property pervades the foundation of social improvement. It leads to the cultivation of the earth, the institution of government, the establishment of justice, the acquisition of the comforts of life, the growth of the useful arts, the spirit of commerce, the productions of taste, the erections of charity, and the display of the benevolent affections."

Kent believed that "human society would be in a most unnatural and miserable condition" if it would follow the speculations of the modern theorists who consider inequalities in property and the right to "separate and exclusive" property as the cause of injustice, and of the "unhappy result of government and artificial institutions."

The term "property," like the terms "life" and

"liberty," is also a representative term. It carries with it as its natural and necessary coincident all that effectuates and renders complete the full, unrestrained enjoyment of that right. Within its comprehensive scope are embraced—as our courts have explained—every auxiliary right, every attribute necessary to make the principal right to property effectual and valuable in its most extensive sense. No person shall be deprived of his property rights by an arbitrary power in any form. Where rights of property are admitted to exist, neither the legislative, executive, nor judicial agencies can declare they shall exist no longer. Prohibition, regulation, or interference with the right to property can be upheld only under the police power rightfully exercised for the protection of the public safety, the public health, or the public morals.

Blackstone defines the term "police" as "the due regulation and domestic order of the kingdom, whereby the individuals of the state, like members of a well governed family, are bound to conform their general behavior to the rules of propriety, good neighborhood, and good manners, and to be decent, industrious, and inoffensive in their respective stations." The state's or municipality's authority to enact legislation for the protection of the public safety, the public health, or the public morals grows out of what is known as its "police power." This power is inherent in every sovereignty to govern men and things under which the legislature may within constitutional limitation prescribe regulations to promote the public health, morals, and safety and add to the general public prosperity and welfare.

Of course, the regulations cannot be unreasonably arbitrary or capricious.

Police power regulates the use of property or impairs rights in property when free exercise of these rights is detrimental to public interest. Appropriation of property takes place for the purpose of destruction when it is dangerous or by the way of confiscation as a penalty. When the property is dangerous, it is not taken for public use but for destruction in order to promote general welfare. Protection of life is of greater importance than the protection of private property rights. The owner is not compensated for any damage he may sustain since he is sufficiently compensated by sharing in the general benefits resulting from the exercise of the police power.

Police power and eminent domain have been sometimes confused. Eminent domain power is the right of the government acting in the interest of the public to force the owner of the property to sell the same to the public. The constitutions adopted by the states and the Fourteenth Amendment guarantee the owner fair and adequate compensation and due process. Eminent domain takes property because it is useful to the public. The "public purpose" is viewed in the light of technical development and economic and social conditions. When public need requires the acquisition of private property, eminent domain power protects the public from being deprived of the needed public service if the owner refuses to sell his property or from paying an excessive price demanded by an owner.

The state or municipality takes property under the

eminent domain power because it is useful to the public, and under police power because it is harmful or it is the cause of the public detriment. The destruction of property to avert impending peril, as to prevent the spread of fire, is an exercise of the police power. Taking of property for the building of roads, streets, highways, water reservoirs, hospitals, and schools and for many other services meeting the needs of the public is an exercise of the eminent domain power. Police power when exercised within its legitimate limits requires no compensation, whereas eminent domain recognizes a right to compensation. Both powers enable government to carry out the purposes for which they were organized under the respective federal and state constitutions.

Both powers are founded in public necessity, and only public necessity can justify their exercise. Arbitrary legislation which passes under the guise of the police power is void. Also void is any legislation if it serves no useful purpose to advance public welfare or if the restriction of private rights is oppressive and the public welfare is enhanced only in slight degree. The Constitution permits no excessive encroachment upon the private right of property. Only the attainment of some public object of sufficient necessity and importance can justify the exertion of these powers. Private rights to property should never be sacrificed to a greater extent than necessary. The fundamental maxims of a free government do not leave the rights of property solely dependent upon the will of the legislative body, nor would any court of justice in this country be warranted in assuming an arbitrary power to violate and disregard the right to property, which should be held sacred.

Political Significance of the Trinity of Rights

As mentioned earlier, these are rights in every society which are beyond the control of the government. When on April 25, 1775, the people of Philadelphia received the news of the Battle of Lexington, the bell called together over 8000 patriots whu assembled in the Statehouse yard and agreed unanimously "to associate for the purpose of defending with arms, our lives, liberty, and property against all attempts to deprive us of them."

The trinity of rights encompasses a broad group of rights recognized in a free society to which we have referred before, namely the right to be free from governmental violations of the integrity of the person—violations such as torture; cruel, inhuman, or degrading punishment; invasion of the home; arbitrary arrest or imprisonment; and denial of public trial. Among the numerous reflections of the right to liberty, we may list the right to follow one's conscience; the right to enter into contracts and to acquire and to enjoy property; the right to travel freely within and outside one's own country; the right to be free from discrimination based on race, religion, or sex; and the right to enjoy civil and political rights, including freedom of speech, press, religion, and assembly.

We have referred to rights in a "free society," not in a "democracy"—although in the past the terms have been used almost interchangeably—because on the contemporary international stage we find many governments fraudulently using the terminology of democracy or of "people's democracy." The totalitarian regimes fraudulently refer to the people as a source of their legitimacy, and their constitutions, elections, and representative assemblies are meaningless. The dictator and the political party in power reject in principle the idea of human rights and rule through a massive bureaucratic and police apparatus. Efforts to create freer and more pluralistic societies are met with tanks, imprisonment, torture, and exile.

The rights to liberty, life, and property are "inalienable." The Declaration of Independence states, "To secure these rights, governments are instituted among men, deriving their just powers from the consent of the governed." The rights of the individual are not derived from governmental agencies, or even from the Constitution. They exist by the endowment of the Creator, and are merely reaffirmed in the Constitution. The government's authority comes from the people. In other words, we are self-governing people, and our government was not designed to be paternal in form.

Our entire social and political structure rests upon the cornerstone that all men have certain rights that are inherent. These natural rights may not be transgressed with impunity nor disregarded because of expedience; neither may they be abrogated, abridged, or suspended by any human enactment because they are based on "the laws of nature and of nature's God," on truths which are "self-evident." The self-evident truth, we repeat, is that "all men are created equal, that they are endowed by their Creator with certain inalienable rights."

CHAPTER III

DUE PROCESS OF LAW

History of Due Process of Law

The right to due process of law rests on the Fifth Amendment to the Constitution, ratified on December 15, 1791, and on the Fourteenth Amendment, ratified on July 23, 1868. The first is binding on the federal government, the second binding on the states. Both amendments command that no person shall be deprived "of life, liberty, or property without due process of law." Although no concept is raised more frequently in our judicio-legal process, especially in appellate cases at the level of the United States Supreme Court, the phrase "due process" has never achieved an exact definition. The Constitution contains no description of those processes which it was intended to allow or forbid. Neither does it declare what principles are to be applied to ascertain whether any particular procedure is due process.

The concept of due process of law has historical roots of ancient origin. Its existence does not depend upon any statute or constitutional provisions. It had been interwoven in the common law long before the adoption of the Magna Charta. It was not alien to the Justinian Code which survived the Roman empire and which has given us one of the fundamental maxims of justice, *suum cuique tribuere* ("to render every man his due").

105

The history of the due process of law and of the law, broadly conceived, is the history of civilization and of mankind itself. Man has always recognized the need for a body of rules which could regulate his and his fellowman's actions—acknowledging, in that need, that he was at once prone to error in his relations to others and subject to some higher standard of judgment. Every civilization of which there is a record is governed by some sort of law, in the sense of a mandatory system enforced by power. Even before a written code of law, we find not anarchy but some system of rules.

It is necessary to distinguish betwen societies in which there is indeed law to protect men from one another (all societies have such provisions in one form or another) and those in which the individual has within the law itself standards of protection from society's abuse of its power over him. Most societies we call primitive have no such standards. These usually come only after—sometimes a long time after—the introduction of a written body of laws. We must also distinguish between "law," a generally understood body of rules that govern social behavior, and "laws," specific regulations promulgated by some central authority, whether a king or a legislature or a whole people voting together as in a Greek city-state. The desired end of law is justice, and it was often felt—for instance in Greece—that justice resided in the traditional law handed down from generation to generation and often not written down.

The great lawgivers, like Hammurabi and Moses, did not invent law, they merely articulated it. Hammurabi's Code, which is the earliest system of laws to have become generally known to most people, is in turn based on earlier legal systems in the Tigris-Euphrates valleys; these, no doubt, had their own predecessors. Moses, even after communing with God on the mountain of Horeb, did not bring back to mankind a revelation utterly new. The core of the Mosaic law is the natural law that God had already written on the hearts of men. There were new elements, to be sure, in the blazing insistence on loyalty and obedience to the monotheistic deity who had chosen the nation of Israel and in the special regulations that were designed to mark off that nation as a separate and consecrated people.

In Greece, the classic lawgiver in Athens, the equivalent of Hammurabi or Moses, was Solon. Little direct evidence remains of the substance of the legal code which he drew up. Scholars, however, have surmised that it represented a new standard of due process and equal protection of all. As far as the record goes, he was the first statesman on the European scene who proclaimed impartial protection for the noble and the commoner, the wealthy and the poor, the powerful and the powerless. In spite of the wide dimension of Solon's thoughts and projected program, the State remained omnipotent, and individual liberty, giving rights against the city and its gods, did not exist. The citizen had political rights to vote, to name magistrates, to have the privilege of being archon, but because of the sacred and religious character with which society was clothed, the Greeks stressed the importance of the rights of the State.

To the southeast across the Mediterranean, even more than the thought of Greece, the Hebrew tradition was preeminently sacred and religious in character. But because of its devotion to the idea of the law as a written and unchangeable code—modified and elaborated upon first by oral tradition and then by written exegesis but always bound by the central revelation—Judaism contributed much to our sense of the protection afforded by due process of law.

We may take for an example the elaboration of the Judaic law on the matter of witnesses to testify. Although several brought witness against Jesus, their testimony did not hold up because of discrepancies. (Mark 14:57.) (It was only when the Priest questioned him: "Are you the Messiah, the Son of the Blessed One?" that Jesus replied, "I am," and went on to explain for what confirmation to look for.) In Jewish laws, a witness convicted of swearing falsely had to bear the penalty that would have been inflicted on the accused. (Deuteronomy 19:16-19.) The evidence of at least two witnesses was required for convicting an accused person (Numbers 35:30 and Deuteronomy 17:6 and 19:15.)

These basic requirements never changed, but they were refined in Rabbinic tradition. By the twelfth century, Maimonides could list ten classes of persons who were not competent to testify. Rules of inquiry, investigation, and interrogation evolved out of the biblical injunction, "Thou shalt then inquire and make search and ask diligently." Complex rules developed as to how to decide between conflicting groups of witnesses who contradicted each other in sworn testimony. Because of its profound respect for law as God-given and because of the unchangeable and unchallengeable basic rights and procedures laid down in the Torah, Judaic law afforded one of the earliest examples of procedural protection of human rights.

Under Roman law, the idea of citizenship implied the defense of individual rights against the unbridled power of the State. Roman citizenship meant liberty protected by law throughout a vast empire. At first restricted to patricians of Rome itself and later extended to certain plebeians, over the years the possibility of acquiring citizenship became a reality for many inhabitants of the Roman empire. When the Jews of Jerusalem seized the Apostle Paul and tied him up to be flogged, he asked the centurion who was standing there, " 'Can you legally flog a man who is a Roman citizen, and moreover has not been found guilty?' " The centurion "reported it to the commandant . . . and the commandant himself was alarmed when he realized that Paul was a Roman citizen and that he had put him in irons." (Acts 22:25-26, 29.) When the Roman governor Festus later asked Paul whether he was willing to be returned to Jerusalem for trial, Paul said, " 'I appeal to Caesar.' Then Festus, after conferring with his advisors, replied, 'You have appealed to Caesar: to Caesar you shall go.' " (Acts 25:11-12.).

Roman law served as a model for many centuries and still provides the basis for the legal systems of many nations of the world—largely because its provisions provided a bulwark of law and justice for its citizens. Except for its survival in some aspects of

Canon Law, the Roman law was largely forgotten in Medieval times. The peoples who grew into the modern Western European nations evolved their legal systems out of tribal and later feudal law.

Many of the provisions of these systems seem incomprehensible to us. The concepts, for instance, of trial by battle or trial by ordeal (such as by fire or by water) are to us barbaric miscarriages or perversions of justice. In their own times, however, such provisions of the law might have even seemed enlightened or merciful. The courts were not places where due process of law or impartiality could be taken for granted; perjury was common and procedural remedies to prevent or disprove it were doubtful. Sometimes abandoning one's case to the proof of one's own might or to the providence of God was the last resort if justice indeed was to be done. The leading British historian of the law, Sir William Holdsworth, comments:

> "The age was superstitious, and miracles were plentiful because they were believed. It did not appear absurd to hope that God would protect the right. But it was also an age of corruption; and in a really corrupt age it is easier to meet a perjured claim by more detailed and particular perjury than to establish the truth. Battle, ordeal, and compurgation were suited to the age in which they flourished. Growing civilization demanded a clearer and more certain test." (Holdsworth, *A History of English Law*, Volume I, 7th Ed., Methuen & Company, 1956, pp. 311-312.)

In looking back over the history of the ages, it was the Magna Charta that provided a more orderly and deliberate method of protecting natural human rights.

Law of the Land

It is well settled that under modern law the phrases "due process of law" and "law of the land" are interchangeable and identical in import. The Magna Charta, called the "palladium of English liberty," in its thirty-ninth clause provides that no free man may be imprisoned, outlawed, exiled, condemned, or in any way destroyed, unless according to the law of the land. Concerning the expression "the law of the land," Lord Coke—one of the most eminent jurists in the history of England, whose doctrines of individual liberty had a profound effect on history—pointed out in his commentary on the Magna Charta that the Charter does not specify the "laws and customs of the King of England, lest it might be thought to bind the King only, nor the people of England, lest it might be thought to bind them only, but that law might to extend to all, it is said 'by the law of the land,' *i.e.* England." He continues:

> "The law is the highest inheritance which the King hath, for by it the King and all of his subjects are ruled, and, if the law were not, there should be neither King nor inheritance. The Kings of England have always claimed a monarchy royal, not a monarchy signoral. Under the first, the subjects are freemen, and have a propriety in their goods and freehold in their lands, but under the

latter they are villeins and slaves; and, my lord, this propriety was not introduced into our land as the result of princes' edicts, concessions, and charters, but was the old fundamental law, springing from the original frame and constitution of the realm."

In other words the rule that a person shall not be deprived of life, liberty, or property without an opportunity to be heard in defense is a fundamental right existing prior to the adoption of the Magna Charta. This rule is founded on the principle of natural justice and natural rights. Every person in the enjoyment of his natural rights has an inherent right to due process of law, which protects the citizen against all mere acts of power, whether flowing from the legislative or the executive branch of government.

Due process of law means, therefore, something more than the actual existing law of the land, for otherwise it would be no restraint upon legislative power. The question arises: To what principle are we to resort to ascertain whether any legislation or any governmental act is contrary to the prohibition of the Constitution as to due process of law? The Supreme Court of the United States has offered a twofold answer. First, we must examine the Constitution itself to see whether the act is in conflict with any of its provisions. If not found so, we must look "to these settled usages and modes of proceeding existing in the common and statute law of England before the emigration of our ancestors, and which are shown not to have been unsuited to their civil and political conditions by having been acted on by them after the settlement of this country."(*Den v. Hoboken Land and Improvement Co.*, 18 How. 372, 374 [1856].)

Does it mean that a process of law which is not otherwise forbidden can be regarded as due process of law only if it is sanctioned by the settled usage both in England and in this country? An affirmative answer would deny law the capability of progress or improvement. The cardinal principles of justice are immutable, but the methods by which justice is administered are subject to fluctuation. Each generation originates important reforms. Law draws its inspiration from new experiences, and the administration of justice changes with the progress of society and the advancement of legal science. The spirit of individual rights can be preserved by progressive growth of the law through adaptation to new circumstances and developments.

The Magna Charta gave the barons guarantees against the oppressions and usurpations of the King's prerogative, but did not limit the power of parliament, which was controlled by the barons. Because of the omnipotence of the parliament, arbitrary acts of legislation were not regarded as inconsistent with the law of the land. While in England the only protection against legislative tyranny was the power of free public opinion represented by the Commons, our Bill of Rights puts limitations upon the powers of the three branches of government, legislative as well as executive and judicial.

The maxims of justice and individual freedom of our law of the land perform a different function from the concessions of the Magna Charta that were wrung from the King. Our law of the land is designed to serve as a bulwark against all arbitrary acts of power and not only against executive despotism. The prohibitions of the Fifth and Fourteenth Amendments apply to all instrumentalities of the government, to its legislative, executive, and judicial authorities.

In the significant case of *Hurtado v. People of the State of California* (110 U.S. 516 [1884]), the Court held that due process of law in the Fifth Amendment refers to the law of the land, which derives its authority from the legislative powers conferred upon Congress by the Constitution of the United States, exercised within the limits therein prescribed, and interpreted according to the principles of the common law. In the Fourteenth Amendment, the due process of law refers to the law of the land in each state, which derives its authority from the reserved powers of the state, that include the fundamental principles of liberty and justice inherent in the very idea of free government and of the inalienable rights of a citizen in such a government.

Then the Court follows with this definition of due process of law.

"Any legal proceeding enforced by public authority, whether sanctioned by age and custom, or newly devised in the descretion of the legislative power in furtherance of the general public good, which regards and preserves these principles of liberty and justice, must be held to be due process of law."

Legal procedure may be changed from time to time, but always with due respect to the landmarks of liberty and justice established for the protection of the citizen. Due process of law is, however, more than legislative provisions merely providing forms and modes of attainment with no power over the substance of justice. Due process is founded on the essential nature of individual rights, which are not limited to life, liberty, or property. As Justice John Marshall Harlan pointed out:

> "When the Fourteenth Amendment forbade any State from depriving any person of life, liberty, or property without due process of law, I had supposed that the intention of the people of the United States was to prevent the deprivation *of any legal right* in violation of the fundamental guarantees inhering in due process of law. [Emphasis added.]" *(Taylor v. Beckham,* 178 U.S. 548, 599, 20 S. Ct. 890, 1014 [1899].)

The meaning of the Fourteenth Amendment was highly debatable. Some, like Jusice Black, believed it incorporated all the guarantees embodied in the Bill of Rights. Others, and among them Justices Frankfurter and Harlan, advocated the concept that this Amendment incorporated fundamental values which may or may not be included in the Bill of Rights. The recent decisions of the United States Supreme Court call for the enforcement of the fundamental constitutional rights against the state's encroachment by the same standards that are applied against federal encroachment. Thus, for instance, the privilege against self incrimination of the Fifth

Amendment is applicable under the Fourteenth
Amendment; the Fourth Amendment's standards
concerning unlawful search and the Sixth Amendment's provision of right to counsel are fully applicable to the states. Identical prohibitions against the
estabishment of religion or against abridging freedom of speech and the free exercise of religion are
applicable to both the federal and state governments.

The guarantee of due process of law is absolute
and not merely relative. It asserts a fundamental
principle of justice rather than a specific rule of law,
and thus is not susceptible of more than a general
statement. Because the influence of constantly
changing economic, political, and social forces is a
vital factor in the interpretation of due process of law,
its meaning has never been fixed and invariable in
content. As a historic and generative principle, due
process of law precludes definition. It is not surprising that in the Supreme Court some members have
denounced decisions of the majority of their fellow
Justices, particularly in regard to procedural due
process, as "dangerous experimentations" offering
"a balance in favor of the accused." A test offered
by Justice Frankfurter based on a case-by-case
approach—"Does this conduct shock the conscience?"—met with heavy criticism. Justice Black
described Frankfurter's opinion as "merely high-
sounding rhetoric void of any substantive guidance
as to how a judge should apply the Due Process
Clause." (A *Constitutional Faith*, Alfred A. Knopf,
1968, pp. 29-30.)

There is a general consent that due process of law
should not be regarded as the equivalent of custom-

ary legal procedure since it is not limited to checking on departures from procedural regularity. It should also be conceded that it has never achieved, even in the field of "personal rights," a precise meaning. Because of the towering disagreements as to its meaning, the importance of the concept of due process of law can be realized only by weighing it against concepts of a legal system that disregards the basic standards of due process of law.

Legal System Without Due Process of Law

Marx believed that the legal system has a historical dimension and that, in accordance with the principles of historical materialism, the contents of laws and of legal institutions conform with the material interest of the ruling class. Thus economic relations determine the subject matter comprised in each juridical act. The Bolshevik revolution, therefore, sought to abolish the existence of law by destroying the old courts created by the czarist regime and by creating people's courts not bound by the law and conceived by the overthrown government. The judges were to be guided by their "revolutionary consciousness"; law was stigmatized as a tool of bourgeois exploitation.

In its first phase, communism, according to Marx and Lenin, cannot be fully developed economically and "entirely free from traces of capitalism." Marx admitted the inevitability of defects during the transformation of society from a capitalist basis to a socialist one. In the first phase of communist society, when it "has just emerged after prolonged birth pangs from capitalist society," the capitalists' standard of "right" will not disappear at once. With an equal performance of labor, one may receive more than others and one will be richer than another. These defects, states Marx, will disappear in the higher phase of communist society when the "narrow horizons of bourgeois right" will be transcended entirely and society will inscribe on its banners: "From each according to his ability, to each according to his needs."

Lenin defined dictatorship as "a power basing itself on coercion and not connected with any kind of laws." He goes further than Marx, however, when he argues that under communism there "remains for a time not only bourgeois right but even the bourgeois state—without the bourgeoisie." Since "law is nothing without an apparatus capable of enforcing it," he sees the need for a State which, while safeguarding the public ownership of the means of production, "would safeguard equality in labor and equality in the distribution of products."

Stalin and his followers went still a step further than Lenin by arguing that dictatorship of the proletariat, which is crucial in the period of revolutionary transformation, creates a State of a new type that in turn creates a new type of law—the Soviet democratic law. Proletarian dictatorship calls for the omnipotence of State power and for a law that will safeguard the new revolutionary mechanism of State authority and protect the interest of the toilers. Stalin rejected the concept of the gradual withering away of the State and the law. The stability of the laws, he declared, "is necessary for us now more than ever."

Stalin's constitution of 1936 implies the reinforcement rather than the withering away of the law.

Evgeny B. Pashukanis, one of the leading authorities in Soviet legal science after the Bolshevik revolution, rejected the idea of "proletarian law." Law, he maintained, is peculiar to bourgeois society and has its origin in commodity exchange. Since socialism will bring about the abolition of commodity exchange, the law will disappear together with the State. Devoted to his commodity exchange theory of law, which he identified with the Marxist theory of law, he predicted that private law will wither away when the institutions of private property and of market conditions have been eliminated. He thought that socialism should not impart a new content to the law, and found no reason to replace the bourgeois law with a new proletarian one. In 1937 he was liquidated by Stalin as a "legal nihilist" and as a member of the "Trotsky-Bukharin fascist agents." This fate was shared by others who adhered to the Marxist dogma of the abolishment of law.

The Stalinists rejected the "bourgeois" concept of due process of law. The purpose of their new law was to "smash the bourgeois state machine" and to inflict "a death blow on bourgeois law." There is no place for due process of law when the fundamental principles of liberty and justice which lie at the base of all our civil and political institutions are denied. The concept of due process of law as the observance of individual rights and protection against the arbitrary exercise of government power is diametrically opposed to the idea of the dictatorship of the proletariat. Stalin defined such a dictatorship at the

XVIth Party Congress as "the highest development of state authority." It "represents the most potent and mighty authority of all State authorities that have existed down to this time."

Under such a dictatorship, the court is an instrument of the party and the judicial process is subordinated to the political end of assuring revolutionary order and the authority of the State. Such law expressed the fundamental principle of State dictatorship, and the judicial process is used to legalize the terror applied by the State and its secret police. It is in the interest of the party and the ruling authority of the State to sanction political terror within the context of formal legalism; the main function of the judicial process is to protect the dictatorship from any kind of interference. The court is thus merely an instrument of the party in power.

Stalinist Order

What were the results of this kind of administration of justice? Stalin used it as one of the chief weapons in establishing the revolutionary order by the elimination and destruction of anybody who might hamper the building of the "socialist order." The word "might" should be emphasized, because under this system of contempt for due process of law a person could be charged with a hypothetical offense against the socialist order.

In the time of the great purges, the concentration camps were filled with prisoners arrested on grounds of being "potential spies" simply because they had been outside the country. It was unimportant they were sent abroad on a government mission; the important part was that, having spent a period of time in a foreign country, after their return they "might" have been "potential spies." Similarly, the concentration camps were filled with prisoners charged with being "socially dangerous." Stalin's "legal order" was first of all concerned with the relationship of class domination. The protection of the interest of the dominant class of toilers permitted the oppression of all elements which "potentially" could be opposed to the socialist system.

Under this system of punishing "potential" wrongdoers, not only violators of the new order were punished, but also the "indifferent" and the "passive," those who did not manifest affection for the new "morality," the new customs, the new ideas, the new Stalinist order. Such persons were regarded as dangerous to society; in concentration camps, the omnipotent State tried to "refashion" their intellects and consciences by destroying their old "prejudices," habits, and attitudes which did not benefit the ruling party's concept of the State order.

The axiom of the infallibility of the communist program is accompanied by the responsibility of "somebody" for its failures. In the 1932-1933 years of severe famine, the mass arrest of farmers took place as punishment for their failing to achieve the results of the economic plans approved by the party. The scarcity of food was explained by their "reactionary activity to undermine the security of the Soviet Union." The arrests were followed by confessions of sabotage. Tortures were inflicted to coerce the prisoners to confess to crimes they had never committed.

The mass arrests were chiefly organized in order to attain either or both of two goals: first, to convince the people that the communist party was perfect and that all economic failures were only a result of "subversive activity of the enemies of the Soviet people"; second, to supply forced labor on a massive scale.

Most of the major public works, including highways, railroads, canals, and tunnels, were built on the bones of millions of prisoners. In 1937 millions of innocent victims of Stalin's great purge were arrested and died in the camps. To supply labor, for instance, for the Moscow-Volga Canal, some of the victims were arrested under the charge of being a "socially dangerous element," proved by the fact that they had already been convicted once in the past. They were jailed to furnish unpaid labor under subhuman conditions, with no need to provide the minimum of goods which free workers expect.

Millions of people were transported to enforced labor camps from European areas occupied during the war by the Soviet Army, as well as from the Soviet areas liberated from the German occupation. Whoever survived the German occupation was a potential collaborator with the emeny. The population of the "liberated" republics was transported in "echelons" (cattle trains especially adjusted for mass exile) to the far north. They were simply sent there to furnish unpaid labor.

The family members of "politically dangerous" citizens were also subject to reprisals. The recently published *The Correspondence of Boris Pasternak and Olga Freidenberg 1910-1954* (Elliot Mossman, Ed., Harcourt Brace Jovanovich, 1982) reveals that

Olga Ivinskaya, with whom Pasternak had fallen in love, served two terms in a concentration camp because of her association with Pasternak. Pasternak's cousin Sasha died in the camps, and Sasha's wife Musya was also arrested. Pasternak's brother, Alexander, who for his work as designer and supervisor of the construction of the Moscow-Volga Canal received a medal from Soviet Chairman Mikhail Kalinin, rejected pleas that he petition the release from camps of some of his family members.

In the atrocity and horror of holocaust, Hitler runs a distant second to Stalin, who was responsible for the deaths of 20 to 50 million of his countrymen. Stalin was shrewder than Hitler was. Both of them inflicted upon millions of people brutal methods of extermination and of systematic moral and physical tortures. But Hitler murdered and persecuted to destroy nations and races; Stalin destroyed his "enemies" and "potential enemies" after exploiting to the utmost limit their ability to work. The concentration camp later or sooner became their tomb, but before their death, as long as they were healthy and strong, they had to give their strength to the State.

The Soviet Union won World War II. It annexed the Baltic countries and extended its control over Eastern European countries by establishing puppet governments, a method that had also been used by the Nazi invaders. But the Soviet Union shared with the Nazis a defeat in the battle for human minds. The war raised the Iron Curtain and revealed the communist theater of cruelty directed by a psychotic master who caused the deaths of millions of citizens. In the postwar period, numerous books and movies described the Nazi concentration camps. The details of Stalin's system of mass death now became available through the writings of Russian emigrés, to mention only Solzhenitzyn's *The Gulag Archipelago* and Antonow Ovseyenko's *The Time of Stalin: Portrait of Tyranny*. (The author is the son of one of the heroes of the Bolshevik revolution whom Stalin had killed.)

The horrors of the Nazi holocaust have received ample attention from the producers of television documentaries; not so the Soviet horrors. In May 1982, CBS broadcast a movie called "Coming Out of the Ice," about a U.S. citizen who spent ten years in Siberian concentration camps. The movie, an almost unprecedented event in the history of television, told the story of Victor Herman, who in 1931 came with his parents to Russia to work in Ford's automobile plant in Gorky. As an exceptionally talented athlete he set a world parachute-jumping record. When toward the end of the decade the contract with Ford lapsed, Herman wanted to return to the United States. The Russians refused to let him out, since he refused to sign a document attesting that his athletic record was set by him as a Soviet citizen. He spent ten years as a prisoner in a slave-labor camp.

The broadcast based the details of the life in a labor camp on first-hand observations of Russian writers such as Solzhenitzyn, Ginsburg, and others, who in their memoirs have given a poignant account of life in the camps. The scenes—of Herman beaten up by the Russian interrogators for his refusal to acknowledge Soviet citizenship; of him receiving from his friend, who is being sent farther north, a trap that will give him a chance to survive by eating the rats it catches; of a dead man in a latrine covered with rats; and of a boxcar from which the guards pushed female prisoners to be raped by the male prisoners deserving "entertainment"—explained the true nature of a system that consumes its own citizens.

These scenes give a better understanding than any legal definitions of the significance of our constitutional individual rights and the importance of the guarantees provided by the due process of law clause. These scenes based on the testimony of an eyewitness about the life in Soviet concentration camps remind us of the answer given by the American historian, Charles Beard, who when asked if he could summarize the lessons that history teaches, said, "Whom the gods would destroy they first make mad with power" and "When it is dark enough you can see the stars."

In the post-Stalinist era the basic mood of the Soviet people, as described by the famous scientist and winner of the Nobel Prize for 1975, Andrei Sakharov, "is the passivity and indifference of the people induced to drink, burdened and tired by constant economic difficulties." (Sakharov has fallen into official disfavor, was exiled to the city of Gorky in the Russian interior and placed under surveillance.) Forced labor remains an integral part of the Soviet economic system. Although we do not hear about waves of political arrests of the magnitude that swept millions of innocent people under the Stalin regime, and the concentration camps may no longer serve principally to carry out the regime's political repression, the fact remains that the inmates of the labor camps continue to comprise a significant part of the labor force in a country where manpower is in short supply.

Shortages in manpower are solved by increasing the number of people in confinement. Business relations with the Soviet Union may, therefore, mean participation in their repressive system. It is not surprising that voices have been raised saying that in the building the West Siberian gas pipeline the Soviet Union will use the hundreds of thousands of convicted persons who are swept every year into the labor-camp system.

With Due Process of Law

Since the only hope of the people living in the darkness of totalitarian terror is for "the stars to appear," the writers of the Constitution tried to safeguard this country from the darkness of oppression and slavery by providing constitutional guarantees of the rule of due process of law. Although of ancient origin and founded on the principle of natural justice, this rule was enshrined in the Constitution to strengthen the protection of our inherent rights, indispensable to the existence of a free society. This rule, essential to the very concept of justice and ingrained in our national traditions, binds the federal and state governments in every one of its branches, departments, agencies, and other political subdivisions.

The application of this legal, or more accurately, philosophical concept as to the extent to which the State is permitted to exercise its sovereign power, in the last analysis, is a process of judgment by the court. When the controversy is argued before the Supreme Court, the philosophical views of the majority of Justices will decide the presence or absence of due process of law. The impact of the philosophical view of a majority of the Justices is highlighted by a shift of emphasis when personal liberties rather than property rights are involved. That shift has been described by the Court as follows:

> "Thus we find that while in recent years as the Supreme Court has increasingly recognized the right of a state in the exercise of its sovereign power incidentally to deprive individuals of their property, there has at the same time been definitely greater emphasis placed by the court upon the importance of the personal liberties secured to the individual by the Constitution and increased recognition of the place of the due process clause in protecting these liberties from impairment by the state." (*Douglas et al. v. City of Jeannette*, 130 F.2d 652, 658 [1942].)

What the shift of the emphasis means is that the changing interpretation of the Fourteenth Amendment, when applied to the State's exercise of its power inherent in sovereignty (such as police power, taxing power, or eminent domain power), is not intended to hamper the State in effective dealing with growing governmental problems. This shift does not mean, however, that the changing interpretation leaves the State the free play that would permit it to take arbitrary or unjustified action that would deprive individuals of the personal rights secured by the Constitution.

The impact of the philosophical views of the Justices of the Supreme Court, reflected in the changing interpreation of the due process clause, is highlighted by the 5-to-4 decisions in a long list of cases involving the application of the clause to the facts of a particular case. For an illustration, a case involving the religious sect known as Jehovah's Witnesses may serve. The members of this sect sold books and pamphlets without paying the fixed sum required by the city ordinances from all persons following certain specified businesses, trades, or vocations. The members of the sect argued that the ordinance as applied to them was unconstitutional, since it deprived them of their freedom of speech, press, and religion without due process of law. Five Justices construed the ordinance as a proper regulatory measure within the state's police power, to which liberties of the individual should yield. Four Justices interpreted the ordinance as a tax measure, which became—in violation of the due process clause of the Fourteenth Amendment—an instrument to suppress or even destroy the free exercise of speech, press, and religion when applied to the dissemination of educational and religious ideas. (*Jones v. City of Opelika*, 62 S. Ct. 1231, 86 L. Ed. [1943].)

Broadly speaking, the due process clause embodies a standard of fair dealing that satisfies a sense of fairness in every case of the exercise of governmental power. It is not imprisoned within the limits of any formula with a fixed content unrelated to varying circumstances. It is not a technical conception but a process of continued adjustment involving the exercise of judgment based on the experience of the past, sound reason, and the unfailing belief in the strength of democracy and in the sacredness of human rights. This stout belief requires observance of the general rules established in our system of jurisprudence for the security of private rights in any proceedings which may affect these rights.

In observance of these general rules, the Supreme Court has repeatedly stressed that the range of interests protected by procedural due process is not infinite and rejected the notion that "any grievous loss visited upon a person by the State is sufficient to invoke the procedural protections of the Due Process Clause." (*Meachum v. Fano,* 427 U.S. 215, 224, 96 S. Ct. 2532, 2338 [1976].) The application of the clause requires the following analysis: first, to determine whether a decision of the state implicates an individual interest encompassed within the Fourteenth Amendment's protection, always keeping in mind the nature of the interest at stake; second, if the protected interest is implicated, to decide what procedures constitute "due process of law."

For many years after the inclusion of the due process clause in the Fourteenth Amendment it was thought that the due process clause applied only to procedural rights. Gradually, the scope of the clause was broadened, and substantive rights were recognized to be embraced within its protection. The due process of law concept is, therefore, no longer restricted to purely procedural questions but is also involved in political, economic, and social issues that became a matter of judgment in our courts.

Procedural Due Process of Law

Procedural due process—which is the subject of far more litigation than the substantive kind—guarantees every person his day in court, an opportunity to be heard and to defend himself in orderly proceedings adapted to the nature of his case and in accordance with the generally established rules of our system of jurisprudence. To give such proceedings validity, they must be in a court competent by the law of its creation to pass on the subject matter of the case. The right of the person to be present before the tribunal which pronounces judgment upon questions of his life, liberty, or property in their most comprehensive sense must be safeguarded.

A host of practices embraced by a general standard of fairness falls into the category of guaranteed rights and privileges of the individual. Among these are the right to be informed about the nature and the cause of the accusation against him, the right to meet witnesses face to face, the right to counsel in criminal cases, the right to speedy and public trial, protection against self-incrimination, protection against cruel and unusual punishment, protection against double jeopardy, and freedom from unreasonable searches and seizures. These are only some of the examples of our civil rights and liberties that are protected by general standards of fairness and decency. They are firmly implanted in our society and constitute the irreducible minimum of due process of law.

The observance of procedural safeguards, wrote Justice Frankfurter, has largely been the history of liberty. To avoid high-sounding rhetoric, we shall illustrate the application of the concept of due process of law in testing the legality of governmental action by selecting three cases from among the mass of those brought before the Supreme Court of the United States on grounds of alleged denial or abridgement of procedural due process of law.

The first case deals with evidence obtained illegally by forcible extraction of the petitioner's stomach contents. In *Rochin v. California* (342 U.S. 165 [1951]), three officers of the State of California entered the home of a man under suspicion of selling narcotics. When he was asked about two capsules lying on a bedside table, the man swallowed them. After the officers' attempt to remove the capsules forcibly from the man's mouth failed, he was taken to a hospital where an emetic was forced into his stomach against his will. The two capsules were recovered and found to contain morphine, and on this evidence the man was convicted.

The Supreme Court overturned the conviction on the grounds that it was obtained by methods violating the due process clause of the Fourteenth Amendment. The opinion of the court was delivered by Justice Frankfurter, and his primary rationale was that "this is conduct that shocks the conscience." He compared the methods of the policemen to the rack and the screw, and reminded states that there is a general requirement that "their prosecutions respect certain decencies of civilized conduct." To sanction the conduct of the officers "would be to afford brutality the cloak of the law. Nothing would be more calculated to discredit law and thereby to brutalize the temper of a society."

The other case illustrates the sanction of the due process clause against the use of a confession wrongfully obtained—whether under duress by physical force or mental coercion or through illegal means. In *Beecher v. Alabama* (389 U.S. 35, 88 S. Ct. 189, 19 L. Ed. 2d 35 [1967]), the Supreme Court heard a case in which a Negro convict in a state prison had escaped from a road gang. The next day a dead woman was found near the prison camp. The prisoner was captured, tried, and convicted on a charge of first degree murder and given the death penalty. The Court reversed the penalty on the grounds that a preliminary confession was obtained only at gunpoint and that the signed confession was obtained five days later while the man was hospitalized, in intense pain, and under the influence of painkilling drugs so that he was in a "kind of slumber." The conclusion was that the confession was not "free and voluntary" but obtained by the exertion of improper influence.

In the interpretation of the due process clause, we may quite frequently find the Justices of the Supreme Court on a collision course. The case of *Breithaupt v. Abram* (352 U.S. 436, 77 S. Ct. 408 [1957]) may serve as an example. Justice Clark, alluding to the "whole community sense of 'decency and fairness,' " admitted into evidence a blood sample, extracted at the request of law enforcement authorities from the defendant as he lay unconscious. For Justices Black and Douglas, the admittance of such evidence was a violation of the Fifth and Fourteenth Amendments, since the taking of the blood sample was an assault on an unconscious and helpless man.

These three cases serve, among numerous others, as illustrations of the guarantee of due process, which demands that a law shall not be arbitrary or capricious, that the means selected shall have a reasonable and substantial relation to the object sought to be obtained, and that a denial of this guarantee is a failure to observe the fundamental fairness essential to the very concept of justice.

Substantive Due Process

The courts are called upon to take judicial action far less often in the sphere of substantive due process than in the procedural sphere. Substantive due process, as distinguished from procedural rights, refers to the content or subject matter of law. It inhibits the power of the state from depriving a person of life, liberty, or property by an act having no reasonable relation to any proper governmental purpose, or which is so far beyond the necessity of the case as to be an arbitrary exercise of governmental power.

Due process of law inhibits, for instance, the legislative power of the state from taking one man's property and giving it to another person without value received or without any contractual basis. This inhibition is valid regardless of the "merit of glory or value or need of the person on the receiving end of the transaction." A statutory wage-payment-for-voting-time provision, which had the effect of requiring an employer in Kentucky to pay an employee for four hours during which the workers absent themselves on election days to cast their votes, was declared by the court to be unconstitutional. Voting, said the Court of Appeals of Kentucky, is a public enterprise. "But if its maintenance is required by the employer group rather than by the entire, broad general public, then that amounts to a requirement of private maintenance of a public enterprise." *(Illinois Central Railroad Company v. Commonwealth*, 204 S.W.2d. 973, 975 [1947].) (This decision may not reflect the current general state of the law on wage payment for voting time.)

The Supreme Court took a different position in this debatable issue when in 1952, upholding a state law requiring employers to give time employees time off for voting, it stated: "Our recent decisions make plain that we do not sit as a superlegislature to weigh the wisdom of legislation, nor to decide whether the policy which it expresses offends the public welfare . . . [T]he state legislatures have constitutional authority to experiment with new techniques; they are entitled to their own standard of the public welfare." *(Day-Bright Lighting, Inc. v. Missouri*, 342 U.S. 421, 423 [1952].) Justice Douglas explained the attitude of the Court: "The judgement of the legislature that time for voting should cost the employee nothing may be a debatable one . . . But if our recent cases mean anything, they leave debatable issues as respect business, economic, and social affairs to legislative decisions."

The essential concept of substantive due process demands that the state's legislative power, which is broad and useful and extends to all public needs, should not, under the guise of promoting the public interest, arbitrarily interfere with private rights. The state's legislative authority may not unreasonably invade and violate those rights which are guaranteed

under either federal or state constitutions by depriving any person of his property without due process of law.

Another illustration of substantive due process is
sterilization legislation. An Act of Virginia of March
20, 1924, provided that the superintendents of certain health institutions might have sterilization performed upon any patient afflicted with hereditary
forms of mental disease if such an operation were for
the best interest of the patient and of society and if
they complied with the provisions by which the law
protects the patient from possible abuse. The constitutional issue raised before the Supreme Court
was the alleged denial of substantive due process.
The Act of Virginia provided full procedural due
process of law but the appeal to the Supreme Court
contended that sterilization "in no circumstances"
could be justified under substantive due process of
law because a sterilization order is on its face arbitrary, unreasonable, and capricious.

The Virginia statute was upheld by the Supreme
Court. Since the public welfare, reasoned Justice
Holmes, may call upon the society's best citizens for
their lives it would be "strange if it could not call
upon those who already sap the strength of the State
for these lesser sacrifices often not felt to be such by
those concerned, in order to prevent our being
swamped with incompetence." Argued Justice
Holmes: "It is better for all the world, if instead of
waiting to execute degenerate offspring for crime, or
to let them starve for their imbecility, society can
prevent those who are manifestly unfit from continuing their kind." (*Buck v. Bell*, 274 U.S. 200, 207,
47 S. Ct. 584, 585 [1926].)

There are at least two reasons why the Supreme Court has abandoned substantive due process of law as "a perpetual censorship of state legislation." The first one, to which we previously referred, is the change of attitude toward a greater deference to legislatures as the originators of state policy and the guardians of the general welfare. This means that the Court gives more latitude to the state's police power, and exercises greater caution in labeling regulatory statutes as unreasonable, arbitrary, or capricious.

The doctrine of judicial restraint teaches judges to avoid unnecessary lawmaking. One point of view, as explained by Judge Learned Hand, stresses the duty to avoid unnecessary lawmaking in all constitutional cases regardless of whether the cases involve economic or personal freedom. Referring to the constitutional prohibitions, including the ones contained in the First Amendment, Judge Hand wrote: "Indeed, these fundamental canons are not jural concepts at all, in the ordinary sense; and in applications they turn out to be no more than admonitions of moderation." Consequently, the courts should not intervene "unless the action challenged infringes the Constitution beyond any fair dispute." (*The Spirit of Liberty: Papers and Addresses of Learned Hand,* Alfred A.Knopf Inc., 1960, p. 278.)

An opposing point of view rejects Judge Hand's interpretation as foreign to the First Amendment. According to Justice William O. Douglas, the due process clause of the Fourteenth Amendment requires only the legislature to act not without reason and not capriciously. The First Amendment goes much further since it was designed by its framers to take from government the power to decide when freedom of expression may "reasonably" be suppressed. The idea that the prohibitions of the First Amendment are not more than "admonitions of moderation," wrote Justice Douglas, "has done more to undermine liberty in this country than any other single force." (*The Right of the People*, Doubleday & Co., Inc., 1958, pp. 44-45.)

Although there may be no constitutional basis for asserting a larger measure of judicial supervision over "personal" than over economic values, the present position of the majority of Justices of the United States Supreme Court is to give a much stiffer interpretation of the due process clause and a much wider scope for judicial intervention when the subject matter is personal and not economic values.

The Supreme Court has edged closer and closer to the position that the state is free to adopt whatever economic policy may reasonably be deemed to promote public welfare and to enforce that policy adopted to its purpose. The Constitution is not intended to embody a particular economic theory, since it serves people with fundamentally differing views. The judgment of the court should not, therefore, enforce its own abstract notions of the fairness or unfairness of an economic policy. "The courts are without authority either to declare such policy, or when it is declared by the legislature, to override it." (*Nebbia v. New York*, 291 U.S. 502, 537, 54 S. Ct. 505, 516 [1933].)

This position was aptly expressed by the Supreme Court when it stated, "The day is gone when this court uses the Due Process Clause of the Fourteenth

Amendment to strike down state laws regulatory of business and industrial conditions, because they are improvident, or out of harmony with a particular school of thought." (*Williamson v. Lee Optical Co.*, 348 U.S. 483, 488, 75 S. Ct. 461, 464 [1955].) The Court is reluctant to assume the role of a third legislative chamber and prefers to limit its action to keeping the Congress and the state legislatures within their accredited authority. Still, where legislative judgment is oppressive and arbitrary, it will be overridden by the courts. The courts have the right to inquire whether a regulation infringing on individual rights is unreasonable or capricious.

In the area of individual or so-called "personal rights," when legislation collides with the Fourteenth Amendment and also with the First Amendment, the test of legislation is much more definite than the test when only the Fourteenth is involved. This is the second reason for the abandonment by the Supreme Court of substantive due process of law as a check on the infringement of individual rights that fall into the area of First Amendment freedoms. Much of the vagueness of the due process clause disappears when the specific prohibitions of the First Amendment become its standard.

Freedoms of speech, of press, of religion, and of assembly may not be infringed on such "slender ground" as the right of a state to regulate, for example, a public utility. In the latter case, the right to regulate may well include, so far as the due process test is concerned, power to impose all of the restrictions which a legislature may have a "rational basis" for adopting. However, in cases of freedoms falling into the area of the First Amendment, they are susceptible of restriction "only to prevent grave and immediate danger to interest which the state may lawfully protect." It is important to note, stated the Supreme Court, "that while it is the Fourteenth Amendment which bears directly upon the State it is the more specific limiting principles of the First Amendment that finally govern the case." (*West Virginia State Board of Education v. Barnette*, 319 U.S. 625 [1942].)

Equal Protection Clause

In addition to the due process clause, the Fourteenth Amendment contains an equal protection clause. The equal protection clauses of the Fourteenth Amendment and of the state constitutions constitute a guarantee that all persons subject to state legislation shall be treated alike, under similar circumstances and conditions, in privileges conferred and liabilities imposed. There is a tendency to merge the principle of equal treatment to all persons similarly situated with the concept of due process of law into a single guarantee. What is the reason for the vagueness of a distinction between equal protection and due process? The Fifth Amendment contains only a due process clause. Does it mean that the Congress in exercising its power of legislation may deny to persons equal protection of the laws?

To answer these questions we should review the history of the times when the Fourteenth Amendment was passed. Since the early years of the history of this country, the principle of equality has been accorded full recognition by the "law of the land," which was understood to be "a general and public law, operating equally on every individual in the community." Unequal legislation was invalidated by the courts on the ground that it violated the "inherent principles of right and justice," the "natural law," the principles of "natural justice," the "spirit of the Constitition," the decisions "of most respectable judicial tribunals," or the opinions of "learned commentators of the English law."

The incorporation of the Fifth Amendment into the Constitution reflected an already existing inhibition which restrained the powers of the government and asserted the duty of the courts to invalidate legislation inconsistent with consitutional guarantees. These guarantees included the equal protection of the laws. Although the Amendment does not contain the equal protection clause, it does not follow at all that the Congress in exercising its power of federal legislation may deny persons equal protection of the laws. All the guarantees of the Constitution are equal for the benefit and protection of all citizens of the United States.

The equal protection clause in the Fourteenth Amendment was primarily written for the liberated Blacks, although they are not mentioned in the Amendment. To remove the legal doubts about the validity of the Emancipation Proclamation (since it was made under the war power of the President) and to liberate slaves everywhere in the country, the Thirteenth Amendment was adopted. It provides that neither slavery or involuntary servitude shall exist within the United States, or any place subject to its jurisdiction. In practice the Thirteenth Amendment was found to be insufficient. The Supreme Court pointed out that in some states the former slaves continued to be forbidden to appear in towns in any other character than menial servants, that they did not have the right to purchase or own land, that they were not permitted to give testimony in the courts in any case where a white man was a party, and that they were subject to numerous discriminations.

The clause of equal protection of law in the Fourteenth Amendment was designed to prevent a state from making discriminations between its own citizens because of race, color, or "previous conditions of servitude." (See also the Fifteenth Amendment.) Chief Justice Taft made a distinction between due process and equal protection when he explained that "the spheres of the protection they offer are not coterminous." Due process tends to secure equality of law by offering a required minimum of protection for everyone's right of life, liberty, and property. But, writes Justice Taft, "the framers and adopters of this amendment were not content to depend on a mere minimum secured by the due process clause, or upon the spirit of equality which might not be insisted on by local public opinion. They therefore embodied that spirit in specific guaranty." (*Truax v. Corrigan*, 257 U.S. 312, 332, 42 S. Ct. 124, 129 [1921].) Due process, according to Chief Justice Taft, offers a minimum of protection, while equal protection offers a supplemental guarantee. As a supplemental guarantee, the equal protection clause has its own reason for existence and should not be regarded as an incidental right attached to the due process clause.

The Thirteenth Amendment and the two Amendments following were adopted more than sixty years after the first ten Amendments. Because of the experience of the Civil War, restrictions were imposed on the states which before the Civil War would have been impossible. Some of these restrictions were incorporated in the Fourteenth Amendment. In a very few years after the adoption of this Amendment, the docket of the Supreme Court became crowded with cases in which the Court was asked to hold that the state courts and state legislatures had deprived their own citizens of life, liberty, and property in violation of the due process clause of the Fourteenth Amendment.

It is not surprising that the courts were reluctant in the early history of the Fourteenth Amendment to give it a broad meaning. This reluctance was expressed by the Supreme Court when it pointed out that "there exists some strange misconception of the scope" of the due process clause as found in the Fourteenth Amendment and warned that the Fourteenth Amendment should not be viewed "as a means of bringing to the test of the decision of this court the abstract opinions of every unsuccessful litigant in a state court of the decision against him, and of the merits of the legislation on which such decisions must be founded." (*Davidson v. The Board of Administration of the City of New Orleans*, 96 U.S. 97 [1877].)

Because of changes in social values and concerns, the equal protection clause of the Fourteenth Amendment needed implementation to broaden the scope of protection against discrimination based on race, sex, age, creed, and physical handicap. Executive orders issued by our Presidents to curtail such discriminations lacked adequate means of enforcement. (The first such order was issued by President Franklin D. Roosevelt to create the Fair Employment Practices Commission.) The civil rights legislation of the last two decades—to mention only the Civil Rights act of 1964 and the Voting Rights Act of 1965, numerous federal regulations and state laws designed to eliminate discrimination, and the current array of legal measures to promote equal employment opportunity—offers more effective remedies than the equal protection clause of the Fourteenth Amendment against the barriers of discrimination.

Thomas Paine explained the principle of equality when he said: "The principle of equality of rights is quite simple. Every man can understand it, and it is by understanding his rights that he learns his duties; for where the rights of men are equal, every man must finally see the necessity of protecting the rights of others as the most effective security of his own." Advocating the Voting Rights Act at Howard University on June 4, 1965, President Lyndon B. Johnson called for equality not just "as right and theory but equality as a fact and equality as a result." Only the true intention of implementing this principle of equality and the effective enforcement of the guarantee of equal rights may crown with success the long and arduous struggle to put an end to the violations of the founding principle pronounced in the Declaration of Independence. "We hold these truths to be self-evident, that all men are created equal . . ."

Changing Trends

Because of due process and other constitutional guarantees, our homes are safe from unreasonable search on mere suspicion and we are safe from the moral and physical compulsion that wrung confessions from the rack and the screw. The makers of the Constitution undertook to secure conditions to protect Americans in their right to be let alone and in their right to the pursuit of happiness. These rights can be safeguarded only when society's public order is preserved. In accordance with the commands of our democracy and our constitutional principles, our society is also entitled to due process of law. As Justice Cardozo observed, justice "is due the accused, but it is also due the accuser."

Democracy imposes stringent norms restraining the overly zealous collection of evidence, but there is always the danger of shifting the balance in favor of the accused. Some of the decisons of the Supreme Court have become a focal point of attacks by Congress and law enforcement agencies. Dissenting Justices of the Supreme Court have voiced the sentiments of prosecuting authorities when they warned against hampering criminal law enforcement and rendering the task of these authorities "a great deal more difficult." Among the numerous decisions that have attracted heavy criticism for favoring the accused to the detriment of law-abiding citizens victimized by the rising crime in our country are the *Escobedo*, *Miranda*, and *Mapp* cases.

The Sixth Amendment guarantees the right to all persons prosecuted in federal courts to representation by counsel. In dealing with state cases, the Supreme Court considered the education and experience of the accused and the complexity of the charge to determine whether he had been harmed by the denial of counsel. In 1963 the Court repudiated this doctrine by extending the right of indigents to have counsel assigned in all criminal cases. The due process clause of the Fourteenth Amendment made the requirement of the Sixth Amendment of "the assistance of counsel" also obligatory upon the states. (*Gideon v. Wainwright*, 372 U.S. 335 [1963].)

This right to counsel was subsequently in 1964 extended to the preliminary hearing stage. In the famed *Escobedo* case, the Supreme Court reversed the conviction of Danny Escobedo, a young man with a record of numerous arrests who admitted his participation in a murder plot and was sentenced to a twenty-year term in prison, because he was denied the right to consult with a lawyer in the earlier stages of criminal proceedings. Justice Goldberg expressed the five-man Supreme Court majority position when he stated that, when the investigation is no longer a general inquiry into an unsolved crime but has begun a focus on a particular suspect, no statement elicited by police during the interrogation may be used against him at a criminal trial if "the suspect has requested and been denied an opportunity to consult with his lawyer, and the police have not effectively warned him of his absolute right to remain silent." One of the dissenting Justices, Justice Harlan, described this new rule as "most ill-conceived" and expressed concern that "it seriously and unjustifiably fetters perfectly legitimate methods of criminal law enforcement." (*Escobedo v. Illinois,* 378 U.S. 478, 493, 84 S. Ct. 1758, 1766 [1964].)

Two years later, in 1966, the *Escobedo* rule gained further extension to the interrogation stage following arrest. In the *Miranda* case, which has been bitterly criticized and viewed with alarm, the Supreme Court forbade the use of statements made by a person in custody unless he was told that he has the right to have an attorney with him before the interrogation starts. If the person in custody cannot afford an attorney, one must be provided for him free. (*Miranda v. Arizona,* 384 U.S. 436, 86 S. Ct. 1602 [1965].) The *Escobedo* and *Miranda* cases reflected the tide of social change that took place in the 1960s. The current of such change reversed its direction in the 1970s.

In 1971, for instance, Chief Justice Burger held that a statement inadmissible in the prosecution's case chiefly because of a lack of the procedural safeguards required by the *Miranda* case may, if its trustworthiness satisfies legal standards, be used for impeachment purposes to attack the credibility of a defendant's trial testimony. (*Viven Harris v. New York,* 401 U.S. 222, 91 S. Ct. 643 [1971].) In the *Harris* case, the defendant voluntarily took the stand in his own defense. Every defendant is privileged to testify in his own defense, but that privilege cannot be construed to include the right to commit perjury. In the *Harris* case, no warning of a right to appointed counsel was given before questions were put to the defendant when he was taken into custody. However, the shield provided by the *Miranda* decision, stated the Court, cannot be perverted into a license to use perjury by way of a defense, "free from the risk of confrontation with prior inconsistent utterances."

The defendant's credibility can be appropriately impeached by use of his earlier conflicting statement. The *Miranda* decision barred the prosecution from making its case with statements of an accused made while in custody prior to having or effectively waiving counsel. It does not follow, held the Court, that the defendant can turn the evidence inadmissible against him to his own advantage and provide himself with a shield against contradiction of his untruth. The dissenting Justices claimed that the *Harris* decision goes far toward "undoing much of the progress made in conforming police methods to the Constitution." They say a retreat from the *Miranda* case is jeopardizing the privilege against self-incrimination "if an exception against admission of tainted statements is made for those used for impeachment purposes."

As another example of changing trends, the jurisprudence in the application of the exclusionary rule which bars the use of evidence secured through an illegal search and seizure may serve. In 1913, the Supreme Court in *Weeks v. United States* (232 U.S. 383, 34 S. Ct. 341) held that in a federal prosecution the Fourth Amendment barred the use of evidence secured through illegal search and seizure. Since then the federal courts have operated under the exclusionary rule of *Weeks* for almost seventy years. In 1949, the question before the Supreme Court was whether the basic right to protection against arbitrary instrusion by the police demands the exclusion in state courts of logically relevant evidence ob-

tained by an unreasonable search and seizure because, in a federal prosecution for a federal crime, it
would be excluded.

The Supreme Court took the position that in the
Wolf case the rights guaranteed by the Bill of Rights,
comprising the first eight Amendments to the Federal Constitution, are not made applicable to the
administration of criminal justice in state courts by
the due process clause of the Fourteenth Amendment. Consequently, in a prosecution in a state court
for a state crime, the Fourteenth Amendment did not
forbid the admission of evidence obtained by unreasonable search and seizure though the evidence
would be inadmissible in a prosecution for violation
of federal law in a federal court because of a violation
of the Fourth Amendment. The Court stressed that
the security of one's privacy against arbitrary intru-
sion by the police is basic to a free society, but the
choice of the remedy against the violation of the
search and seizure clause is left to the public opinion
of a community, which can effectively be exerted
against any oppressive conduct of the police officers
responsible to the community they serve. *(Wolf v.
People of the State of Colorado,* 338 U.S. 25, 69 S. Ct.
1359 [1949].)

The immediate result of the *Wolf* decision was a
storm of constitutional controversy. There were
those who pointed out that a double standard exists
when evidence inadmissible in a federal court is
admissible in a state court. Since the very essence of
healthy federalism depends upon avoidance of
needless conflicts between state and federal courts,
the critics of the *Wolf* decision asked: Why may a

federal prosecutor make no use of evidence illegally seized, but a state's attorney across the street may, although he supposedly is operating under the enforceable prohibitions of the same Amendment?

Twelve years afer the *Wolf* case, in 1961, the Supreme Court overruled the *Wolf* decision. Justice Clark, who delivered the opinion of the Court, held that the rule excluding illegally seized evidence is of constitutional origin, and, therefore, all evidence obtained by unreasonable searches and seizure in violation of the Fourth Amendment is constitutionally inadmissible in state courts. *(Dollree Mapp v. Ohio,* 367 U.S. 647, 81 S. Ct. 1684 [1961].) "Nothing," wrote Justice Clark, "can destroy a government more quietly than its failure to observe its own laws, or worse, its disregard of the charter of its own existence." In his opinion, Justice Clark referred to the warning of Justice Brandeis: "If the government becomes a lawbreaker, it breeds contempt for law; it invites every man to become a law unto himself; it invites anarchy."

Ten years after the *Mapp* decision, the Supreme Court, in 1971, held that damages may be obtained for any injuries suffered as a result of unreasonable search and seizure by federal officials. *(Webster Bivens v. Six Unknown Named Agents of Federal Bureau of Narcotics,* 403 U.S. 388, 91 S. Ct. 1999 [1971].) This decision enforced further the rule under which law enforcement authorities should be deterred from using improper methods to obtain evidence. The deterrence theory, or exclusionary rule, wrote Chief Justice Burger in his dissenting opinion, "has a certain appeal in spite of the high price society pays for such a drastic remedy." Notwithstanding its plausibility, many judges and lawyers and some of the most distinguished legal scholars have never quite been able to escape the force of Cardozo's statement of the doctrine's anomalous result:

> "The criminal is to go free because the constable has blundered . . . A room is searched against the law, and the body of a murdered man is found . . . The privacy of the home has been infringed, but the murderer goes free!" *(People v. Defore, 242 N.Y. 13, 21, 23-24, 150 N.E. 585, 587, 588 [1926].)*

Justice Cardozo's warning is indeed forceful, but not less forceful is another consideration—the imperative of judicial integrity in the administration of justice and the imperative of constitutional restraints on which the liberties of the people rest. Among these liberties is the right to be secure against unreasonable invasions of privacy by law enforcement officers. The purpose of the exclusionary rule as pointed out by the Supreme Court in another decision "is to deter—to compel respect for the constitutional guaranty in the only effectively available way—by removing the incentive to disregard it." *(Elkins v. United States, 364 U.S. 217, 80 S. Ct. 1444 [1960].)* With this incentive removed, the administration of criminal justice by the federal courts that have operated under the exclusionary rule since 1914 has not been disrupted nor rendered ineffective.

The present U.S. exclusionary rule is not used in most common law countries. They have chosen to admit all evidence, however it is obtained, and to treat the punishment of police officers who have used illegal methods to obtain the evidence as a matter entirely separate from the issue of whether the accused has committed a crime. To protect innocent citizens from illegal search and seizure, offending police officers in some common law countries are punished through internal disciplinary procedures; in others, police officers are held criminally liable for misconduct, and civil damages are assessed against police departments. The punishment of police officers directly is intended to serve as a deterrence against illegal evidence gathering.

Gaining popularity is the idea that the present U.S. exclusionary rule should be modified to include a "good faith exception." Under this exception, a court would not bar the use of highly relevant evidence obtained during an illegal search made in the "reasonable good-faith belief" that it is constitutional. This change would correct the most grievous cases in which criminals get off because of some technical flaw in the conduct of law enforcement officers.

Ordered Liberty

The tide of social change reflects the standards of what, in a free society at a given time, is deemed reasonable and right. These standards do not become petrified as of any one time. In a free society, the courts are expected to enforce the rights that are basic to a free society. Of the fundamental rights, only some have the quality of eternal verity, while others cannot be confined within a permanent catalogue of the essentials of fundamental rights and are subject to the changing conditions developing in a free society. As we discussed above, the present tide has turned in the directions of increased deference to legislative judgment and of growing concern with the upward trend in crime. The remedies offered by the due process clause may, therefore, change from time to time, but always with due regard to the landmarks established for the protection of the citizen and of his security and property.

Decisions under the due process clause, as explained by Justice Frankfurter, require close and perceptive inquiry into fundamental principles of our society. Our administration of justice is based not upon transcendental revelation but upon the conscience of society, ascertained as best may be by a tribunal disciplined for the task and "environed by the best safeguards for disinterestedness and detachment." The faculties of due process may be vague, but the mode of their ascertainment is not "self-willed."

In each case, stated Justice Frankfurter, due process of law requires an evaluation based on a disinterested inquiry pursued in the spirit of science, on a balanced order of facts exactly and fairly stated, on the detached consideration of conflicting claims, on a judgment not *ad hoc* and episodic but duly mindful of reconciling the needs both of continuity and of change in a progressive society. (*Rochin v. California*, 342 U.S. 165, 172, 72 S. Ct. 205, 209 [1951].) As Justice Cardozo twice wrote for the Court, due process of law is a summarized constitutional guarantee of respect for those personal immunities which are "so rooted in the tradition and conscience of our people as to be ranked as fundamental" *(Snyder v. Massachusetts,* 291 U.S. 97, 105, 54 S. Ct. 330, 332 [1933]) or are "implicit in the concept of ordered liberty." *(Palko v. Connecticut,* 302 U.S. 319, 325, 58 S. Ct. 149, 152 [1937].)

The very nature of due process negates any inflexible concept, since it varies with the subject matter and the necessities of the situation. The facts and circumstances of each case may vary, but the purpose of due process never varies—it defines the rights of the individual and delimits the powers which the state may exercise. Its fundamental requirement is to avoid unfairness to individuals resulting from unconstitutional evidence and remedies. In our independent courts was vested the responsibility to resist every encroachment upon the rights stipulated for in the Constitution by its declaration of rights.

In discharging this responsibility it cannot be overlooked that even fundamental rights are not absolute. Decades ago Justice Holmes, referring to the right of free speech, made the famous statement: "The most stringent protection of free speech would not protect a man in falsely shouting fire in a theatre and causing a panic." He referred to the society as "the one club to which we all belong." Above all rights rises our duty to the community and concern about its welfare. In application of the due process clause, the courts have to seek accommodations between individual rights and the people's "concept of ordered liberty." The court draws the line of accommodation by the empiric process of "inclusion and exclusion," by the gradual process that responds to sensible claims by citizens to their rights vital to the maintenance of a free democratic society.

CHAPTER IV

EDUCATION FOR CITIZENSHIP

Two Kinds of Leadership

In the last two decades, educational institutions have not lived up to expectations in providing young people with the education for citizenship that will prepare them adequately to function in a democratic society beset by national and international problems unprecedented in their complexity. In the 1960s, we were faced with growing student disorders that brought about crises on most of the campuses throughout the nation. Some tried to find comfort in the fact that campus unrest is not a new problem, since Plato had written that in a democracy "the schoolmaster fears and flatters the pupils." Others believed that the days of the traditional campus were numbered.

In the 1970s, voices of skepticism accused institutions of learning of being knowledge factories turning out skilled professionals without regard to the traditional aims of liberal education. Our society has the right to expect that educational institutions will discharge their responsibility to prepare good, well-informed citizens, effectively participating in democracy, by exposing students to the moral questions arising in human relations. Such exposure is constructive since only well-informed, educated citizens have the ability to cope with the existing differences between theory and reality when they are faced with such problems confronting our society as the preservation of freedom and justice, the elimination of racial discrimination and poverty, and the search for stability and public order.

Since educational institutions have failed to discharge their responsibility, we have witnessed a taxpayers' rebellion which included resistance to added school taxes and new school bond issues. This taxpayers' "revolt" could be paralled to the resistance of private sources of money whose support was solicited by the private segment of the academic world. The existence of private institutions is being challenged, and a transition from private to public control has occurred in a number of colleges and universities because of financial difficulties. (Between 1968 and 1978, eighty-seven private four-year colleges closed their doors.)

The continued support of taxpayes for public institutions and of private sources for private institutions may depend upon the public's being convinced that our schools, colleges, and universities have not abdicated their responsibility to shape the ideals and habits of our society. As Spinoza expressed it, "Men are not born for citizenship, but must be made fit for it." Because of the relevance of education to the building of a society able to recognize its problems, able to conceive for them effective solutions, and able to put those solutions into effect, we justly may expect that our educational institutions train future leaders responsible to the hopes and aspirations of the mass of people, who in a democracy ultimately shape the nation's destiny. When we refer to future leaders, let us point out two kinds of leadership.

As we look back through the pages of history, we can see that the destiny of the world has been shaped largely by men whose leadership was born in the heat of crisis. From the time of Moses, whose leadership was born in the face of the persecution of the Jews by the Pharaohs, to the present time, leadership has been born in the pain of slavery and exploitation, as a reaction against poverty and misery.

Let us take the history of this hemisphere. The leadership of George Washington would not have been the same had he not faced the crisis of the American Revolution. At age 19, Abraham Lincoln witnessed for the first time the sale of slaves at auctions, and the sight so moved him that he committed himself to abolish the slavery system. Before his resolution could be turned into the action of the Emancipation Proclamation, the entire Unied States had to suffer the crisis of civil war.

Simon Bolivar would not have become the leader he was in South America had he not been faced by the crisis of the exploitation of his compatriots by the Spanish conquerer. In the eyes of many Americans, Woodrow Wilson would not have achieved such great heights of leadership had he not been faced by the crisis of the First World War; nor would Franklin D. Roosevelt have held the great admiration of so many Americans had it not been for the great depression; nor would Dwight Eisenhower have had the same popularity had he not faced the Second World War, which gave him the glory of a victorious general.

We have mentioned some of the world leaders who directed their abilities toward the betterment and the welfare of their societies and the world. If by a leader we mean one who is followed by others in conduct and opinion, we can safely say that some types of leadership which in the course of history have proved to be disastrous were also born in the white heat of crises. Essentially, the conditions that produced the leadership of the *Fuehrer* Adolf Hitler, the *Duce* Mussolini, and the *wozdz* (father of all nations) Joseph Stalin were the same: the economic and political disunity of the people and the hopelessness of the lower classes, who were willing to embrace any idea in an effort to better their conditions.

But there is a second kind of leadership which is greater than that which we have been discussing— greater and different from the leadership of kings and warriors, politicians and dictators—leadership to prevent crisis. There is the leadership of millions who have gone to their graves unknown although they changed the history of the world. We have in mind the leadership of millions who, in their daily life, through their conduct and through their relations to their fellowman, have prevented economic or political catastrophe. To provide this type of leadership which prevents crisis is the primary concern of education for citizenship.

This type of leadership is not founded on birth, wealth, or party membership. As Jefferson pointed out, "There is a natural aristocracy among men. The grounds of this are virtue and talents." This natural aristocracy, which Jefferson believed to be "the most precious gift of nature," calls not for egalitarianism but for vesting the responsibility for our destiny in the hands of educated men and women who excel in intellectual capacity and dedication to their fellow-man.

H.G. Wells, the English sociologist and historian, in his monumental work, *The Outline of History,* pointed out that human history becomes more and more a race between education and catastrophe. What is the role of education in this race to meet the challenge of the dynamically changing world? What is the role of education in the search for leadership to prevent crisis or catastrophe? Whether the miraculous inventions that play such an important part in our society shall be consecrated to man's life or dedicated to his death depends upon the goals we establish for our educational efforts. In establishing these goals it is well to remember the warning Moses gave to the Hebrews: "Behold, I set before you this day a blessing and a curse: the blessing, if you obey the commandments of the Lord your God, which I command you this day, and the curse, if you do not obey the commandments of the Lord your God, but turn aside from the way which I command you this day, to go after other gods which you have not known." (Deuteronomy 11:26-28.)

Benjamin Disraeli in his speech before the House of Commons, June 15, 1874, declared: "Upon the education of the people of this country the fate of this country depends." Since ancient times, the purpose of education has been to make the minds of children fitted to cope with the problems of their environment. Socrates taught that a rightly trained mind would naturally turn toward virtue. The "right training" calls not only for intellectual development but also for spiritual perception in order to understand God's creation of the universe. Growth in knowledge must be joined by growth in grace. Spinoza pointed out the impact of education in the *Ethics:* "One mind, insofar as it understands, is an eternal mode of thinking, which is determined by another mode of thinking and this again by another, and so on to infinity; so they all constitute at the same time the eternal and infinite intellect of God."

Education for citizenship is, therefore, not just an intellectual activity. It shapes the lives of boys and girls, men and women, and illuminates the ways of discharging their responsibilities toward their country and toward world society. Education is not limited to the process of communicating a given skill to successive generations. It also fills the world's spiritual vacuum by bringing divine laws governing the world. Are educational institutions responding to this need? Writing in the fourth century B.C. about the Peloponnesian War, Thucydides stressed the importance of "knowledge of the past as an aid to the interpretations of the future, which in the course of human things must resemble if it does not reflect it." In these times of genuine crisis for institutions of higher learning, much can be learned from recapitulation of educational changes in other countries during this century.

The Monolithic Character of Totalitarian Education

The appearance of Soviet Sputniks in the middle of this century was a great blow to our national pride. The national reappraisal that ensued plunged us into panic, accompanied by an exaggerated upgrading of our estimates of Russian education, training, and achievements. Our former state of blind confidence almost turned into an inferiority complex when we awoke suddenly to the fact that our mortal rival had taken the lead in an area in which we liked to think we excelled—science and technology. Our image of Russians altered radically. Formerly we had pictured Russians as bearded, backward peasants; in the panic brought on by the Sputniks, they emerged as the world's educational leaders, with superior methods of training and preparation. The revelations concerning Soviet educational advances caused a dangerous swing in the pendulum of public opinion to the opposite extreme—just short of admiration for the efficiency of a communist dictatorship. In this admiration, we overlooked the fact that the educational system that exists in Soviet Russia is an admission of the defeat of communist ideas of education, rather than an evidence of their success.

Immediately following the Revolution in Russia, the Soviet schools tried to toss overboard the "capitalist" educational system. The academic and disciplinary responsibility was vested in the hands of councils of pupils; marks, examinations, and the teacher's authority were abolished as an absurdity of capitalist "domination"; teaching by subjects was replaced by crude and dogmatic indoctrination along Marxist lines. The ruling clique, which became the new and merciless exploiting class, gripped control and superintendence over education to wage war on mental concentration. An educated man was dangerous; he could question or protest against slavery, against the horrors and absurdities of the clique that rules through an army of highly paid secret police.

The immediate results of the communist educational philosophy are now well-known; economic disorder, state-planned starvation in concentration camps, and a continued search for scapegoats. All these measures created a lack of skills. Well-trained technicians, specialists, and scientists became scarce in the Soviet Union. In the 1930s, in order to create minds capable of dealing with the growing economic domestic problems and to build a military machine, Soviet Russia abandoned the communist educational principles and returned to the conservative educational methods of their hated capitalist enemy. The switch was simple. The old rigid educational system was again adopted; consequently, marks, examinations, the authority of the teacher, and even the same stern uniforms for school children that date from the time of Catherine the Great were restored. Mandatory job assignments followed graduation. Only a few top-ranking graduates had the privilege of choosing their place of work.

The Marxian goal of a "classless society" without "inequalities of wealth" was forgotten and the highest material rewards were offered for study and mental achievement. The only "contribution" made by the ruling class (the members of the communist party) was the transformation of the schools, all the way from the elementary grades to the most advanced studies, into agencies for state training which closely resemble military agencies of training and mobilization. While education should concentrate on a fully developed human being, the motivating force of Soviet education is to produce a commodity which will best advance their system and establish the U.S.S.R. as a dominant power in the world.

World conquest requires skilled people, and the study of science is the key to power. Languages are needed to expand Russian imperialism and to establish contacts throughout the world. As a state agency, the Soviet school offers pragmatic education with emphasis on immediate utility; it is an education of monolithic character, without the virtues of diversity or the values contributing to intellectual integrity and to the spiritual needs of the individual. This educational system abjures the goal of developing broadly cultured minds and creates instead a trend to replace human thought with a machine-like regimentation. Academic freedom, in the sense that it is practiced in the western world, is unknown.

According to *The New York Times*, the number of Soviet scientists has quadrupled in the past three decades. In 1978, the last year in which comparable statistics were available, there were some 828,100 scientists in the Soviet Union, compared with 595,000 in the United States. The Soviet Union is investing more of its resources in scientific research than any other nation on earth. Some 4 percent of the Soviet gross national product is spent on research, compared with about 3 percent in this country, and Soviet science supplies the Kremlin's needs in many fields, predominantly in the field of war. Eighty percent of the research in the Soviet Union is for military purposes. This scientific underpinning of Soviet military strength may affect the future balance of world power. (Malcome W. Browne, "Soviet Science Assessed as Flawed but Powerful," *The New York Times*, May 20, 1980, p. C 1.)

Experts in the scientific field agree that the average Societ scientist receives an education restricted to his specialty. He is denied access to foreign journals and books, and receives only the technical periodicals published abroad which pass the censor's test. The secret police surrounds and watches the Soviet scientists who attend conferences abroad. In order to satisfy the extreme nationalism of the Russian leaders, the Soviet scientist sacrifices his integrity and dignity by promulgating blatant falsehoods that claim Russian priority in technological inventions and scientific discoveries. By sacrificing his freedom to the State, the Soviet scientist sacrifices also his perception of the wider implications of his work. The price of this sacrifice is a dullness that results from the fact that the State offers no other opportunity for creativity than that which the State itself sponsors. Such creativity has only two goals: the enhancement of military strength and of international prestige.

In totalitarian countries, youths are under the careful guard of the police state and are an integral part of its mechanism. They are taken to meetings, to clubs, to lectures, because only from these "pure sources" can they derive a knowledge of life. A citizen starts with faith in the party or dictator in power and must follow it to the end. With such "training," the future defenders of the regime become "adjusted" so as not to swerve from the pathway marked out for them. They lose the pesonal feeling of direction and meaning of life and their emotions may become similar to the one described by Lord Byron in *The Prisoner of Chillon:*

"My very chains and I grew friends,
So much a long communion tends
To make us what we are:—even I
Regain'd my freedom with a sigh."

Pasternak refers to this kind of Soviet "life adjustment" in his novel, *Dr. Zhivago,* as he described Russia after World War I: ". . . The main misfortune, the root of all the evil to come, was the loss of confidence in the value of one's own opinion. People imagined that it was out of date to follow their own moral sense, that they must all sing in chorus, and live by other people's notions, notions that were crammed down everybody's throat." (Boris Pasternak, *Dr. Zhivago,* Pantheon Books, 1958, p. 404.)

Such evils are not limited to the U.S.S.R., but occur in other totalitarian communist countries as well. In China the policies of Mao Tse-Tung emphasized adherence to the rigid political line of the party with contempt for intellectual achievement and distrust of intellectuals. The so-called Cultural Revolution which took place in Mao's declining years was marked by burning books, by humiliating and beating up professors, and by replacing the academic curricula by manual labor and indoctrination through "political studies."

After ten years of imposed ignorance and the destruction of a generation of educated persons, we can now witness a return to strictly academic standards in China. There are presently about one million students in Chinese institutions of higher education. This figure represents only one percent of the college-age population of the country, compared with almost 50 percent in the United States, where approximately eleven million students are enrolled in institutions of higher learning. Chinese authorities plan to triple the number of university students by 1990. The universities are also trying to reverse the trend of putting heavy emphasis on narrow specialization, which was adopted from the Soviet Union after the communist takeover. During this period, research and development have been neglected and separated from teaching functions. The new curricula now being adopted include basic sciences, foreign languages, management, and humanistic culture.

After the period of anarchy in the system of higher education—a product of the revolution of 1949 and the Cultural Revolution of 1966-1979—the universities are now reintroducing the academic degrees which were abolished by the Cultural Revolution as much resented marks of superiority. Examinations have been reinstated and only the most gifted students are admitted to China's universities. Although some tendencies to hobble the educational process with radical leftish sloganism remain, the Chinese educational system is once again geared to produce competence rather than political orthodoxy. (See Barry Kramer, "China's Educational Revolution," *The Wall Street Journal,* November 27, 1979, p. 24; and Martin and Adam Meyerson, "Reviving China's Universities," *The Wall Street Journal,* September 23, 1980, p. 26.)

Life Adjustment

A different type of life adjustment has been proclaimed in the United States as a goal of education.

This trend in American schools, which stresses method over subject matter, is known as "progressive education" or "learning by doing." The so-called traditionalists believe that this trend is belligerently anti-intellectual. The "progressives," also called "educationalists" or followers of the "Whole Child" doctrine, tell us that their method favoring student-centered rather than subject-centered approaches is the best in the world. When the gap of controversy is so wide, there is always the danger that the facts and estimates concerning our education will fail to break through the crust of consciousness of the American public.

The fact remains that we have witnessed a great revolution in our educational philosophy. From Jefferson's highly selective educational program, which provided that only 20 percent of the best minds should be "raked from the rubbish" annually, we entered into a period during which the existence of differences between the abilities of individuals was not acknowledged. Neither was the aristocracy of subjects acknowledged. Mathematics and mechanics, art and agriculture, history and homemaking all became peers. Scholastic attainment was replaced with scholastic sameness or "togetherness." "What to teach" was replaced by "how to teach"; pragmatic skills replaced intellectual skills—the subject matter of traditional academic disciplines. To require or reward superior intellectual accomplishments or competence was proclaimed to be undemocratic.

Christian ethics, which is a part of our moral standards, does not acknowledge the existence of "rubbish," and proclaims the sacredness of all useful work which serves human needs. At the same time, it provides creative genius with full opportunity of expression and, thus, places before men the vision of man's greatness. In the parable of the talents, the man traveling into a far country gives his servants five, two, and one talent, "to every man according to his several ability." (Matthew 25:15.) All men should have equal opportunities, but all men are not created with equal ability.

All men are born to equal political and civil rights. These rights do not require an egalitarianism offering only mediocrity. The assumption that all men are born with equal powers and faculties is, as John Adams declared, "a gross fraud." The damages caused by egalitarianism are extremely high: students of great ability are deprived of the opportunities to develop their talents; the academic curricula are diluted with proliferating nonintellectual courses; entrance and graduation requirements are weakened or abolished and grades inflated; authority at school and at home collapses; and moral standards, which safeguard society against cultural degeneration and sterility, are rejected.

The program of "life adjustments" offered by "progressive" education judges life in terms of abstract formulas. The followers of this program believe in an egalitarian, productive, and happy society without the help of eternal values by which our moral standards can be measured and compared across time. The idea of "adjustment" deprived of supporting moral force soon deteriorates into the contention that the purpose of "life adjustment" is to educate people to conform to the social conditions surrounding them. In this sense, Jesus, the early Christians, the founding fathers of this country, and the greatest men in history were obviously "maladjusted." Their lives were full of frictions and conflicts with their environment.

Were pain, anxiety, self-sacrifice, crucifixion, and death in the arena of the Roman circus the experiences of "maladjusted" persons? The pioneer circuit riders in this country were undoubtedly "maladjusted" to their environment of gambling, quarreling, and fighting, characteristic of the American frontier. When questioned in a 1976 BBC interview about Bertrand Russell's slogan, "Better red than dead," Alexander Solzhenitsyn said: "In this terrible expression of Bertrand Russell, there is an absence of all moral criteria. Looked at from a short distance this would allow one to maneuver and to continue to enjoy life; but for a long-term view, it will undoubtedly destroy those people who think like that." (*The Listener*, March 4, 1976, p. 261.)

Chief Justice Charles Evans Hughes, in his lecture at Yale in 1910 describing the virtues of citizenship, said, "No one can properly discharge his duties as a citizen who simply has a good-natured feeling towards all . . ." The first duty of a citizen is allegiance to the community and, therefore, he "must learn to make his personal decisions, as well as to define his public attitude, in light of the interests of the community, and not simply with respect to the opportunities for individual gain. No allurement of high salary or of social advantage, no promise of assistance to obtain public office, should be permitted to obscure [one's] duty of absolute loyalty to the public interest."

The European Ivory Tower

There are those who, in reaction to the abuses of progressive education, advocate the complete adoption of an educational standard patterned after the prewar European educational system, with its selectiveness, its sharp division between academic and vocational subjects, and its demands for concentrated efforts in such subjects as mathematics, science, foreign languages, history, and philosophy. But did this educational system pass the crucial tests of citizenship? During the prewar period, graduates of European universities outnumbered all others in Nobel Prize winners in the fields of physics and chemistry, but the same universities faced a most tragic accusation: They failed to recognize their obligation to society. The universities excelled in detailed preparation for a profession, but did not even attempt to come to grips with the vital issues which were changing the destiny of nations, if not the course of the world's history.

The capitulation in prewar Germany of the apostles of universal culture and universal science and the courage of the church to defy the State were pointed out by Reinhold Niebuhr:

"The university was the pride of Germany; and the German church was more or less moribund. Yet the former has allowed its universal culture to be corrupted by the state while the latter has fought valiantly against such corruption. The culture of the university sought universal truth through the genius of the wise man; and forgot that the wise man is also a sinner, whose interest, passion and cowardice may corrupt the truth!" (Reinhold Niebuhr, *Beyond Tragedy*, Charles Scribner's Sons, New York, 1937, p. 284.)

The mundane perspective of prewar European education and its trust in science channeled it into avenues of separation from life. The European universities hoped that the lights in the laboratories would continue to burn while the darkness of oppression surrounded their ivory towers; that the walls of the classrooms would be soundproof against the sirens of the secret police cars and groans of tortured prisoners. They forgot the classic remark attributed to Solon who, when asked how justice could be made secure in Athens, replied, "If those who are not injured feel as indignant as those who are."

With the growing emphasis on technology in this country, we have to be aware of the danger to education for citizenship described by Dr. Henry P. Van Dusen as "The typical American's glorification of the individual, his disdain of the past, his trust in science as mankind's Messiah, his inveterate optimism, his unchallengeable certitude of the fated prosperity and progress of his own nation, his estimate of the true values of life, his delight in gadgets and techniques, his religious unconcern, above all his unshaken confidence in man's power to know and to do—in brief, his this-worldly perspective." (Henry P. Van Dusen, *God in Education*, New York, Charles Scribner's Sons, 1951, p. 50.) Knowledge and trained

skill alone can put blinders on us, blinders that cover
the sight of the central fact of human existence and
exhaust the purpose of life in higher profits, higher
wages, or shorter working weeks. Is this kind of
hedonism the purpose of life? Does the greatness of a
nation lie in its high standard of living or in its high
standard of life?

Both "life adjustment" and "separation from life"
systems of education lack the genuine value of re-
lating education to high standards of life. Horace
Mann in his address in Boston in 1842 stressed the
need of intermingling the principles of science with
principles of morality. "The multiplication tables,"
he said, "should not have been more familiar, nor
more frequently applied, than the rule, to do to
others as we would that they should do unto us." The
question whether the impact of technological
changes will be for good or evil is actually a moral
question. Recognition of eternal values is essential
to the implementation of moral principles, if not to
their very existence. The values to be instilled in our
young by education for citizenship include faith in
the dignity of every individual, honor, duty, belief in
the work ethic, loyalty, and patriotism. The aim of
education for citizenship must not be "life adjustment," not "separation for life," but growth—growth
in the understanding of life.

The sciences do not formulate moral goals, they do
not create a philosophy of life, they do not provide
the final answer to mankind's problems. Scientific
laws describe natural events in terms of cause and
effect but do not explain the purposeful act of Creation of the universe by the Master of Planning. Aris-

totle, who in his *Nicomachean Ethics* wrote that ethics is a branch of politics and that education in morality should be the function of the State, also tried to reach for something beyond human qualities. Even as he wrote that "what is good for a nation or city has a higher, diviner quality" and that the life of the intellect is the best and the most satisfying to man, he added, "Such a life will be too high for *human* attainment. It will not be lived by us in our merely human capacity but in virtue of something divine within us . . ." (*The Ethics of Aristotle*, tr. J.A.K. Thomson, Allen & Unwin, 1953, pp. 15, 275.)

Only when knowledge is used for the growth of persons is a partnership formed between mind and soul. Such a partnership is an evidence of maturity. Spiritual enlightenment enables mental growth, guides the reason's efforts in finding purpose to the creation of the universe. Knowledge combined with moral values is the only force capable of guiding individuals and nations into the social application of conscience, which calls for love and service to fellowman. The union of "truth and love" forms a partnership of mind and soul. Growth in understanding of life calls not only for knowledge of values but also for commitment to them, commitment defined by Cardozo as "submergence of self in pursuit of ideals."

Changing Trends in Education

Each environment, each chapter in the history of civilization, each trend in art or literature has a climate differing in character. When we read in the Old

Testament, we can sense a different atmosphere from that of the New Testament. Socrates, Plato, and Aristotle created a climate conducive to the acquisition of knowledge and to identifying virtue with intelligence, wisdom, and understanding of life's meaning. Two millenia later, Kant startled the world with a new metaphysical system and idealism calling for a new order of democracy and liberty everywhere.

What is the atmosphere, the environment that will tell us of the attitude and character of our universities and colleges? Whether our age will be called the era of "Watergate" or a "New Consciousness," of "Human Rights," or of "Restlessness," history will record that educational institutions were faced with the challenge of fulfilling their social responsibility by undergirding our communities with the strength that derives from educated men and women. What part do educational institutions perform in meeting this challenge for the spiritual and economic well-being of our nation, our communities, and the individual?

After the Civil War, private two-year schools experienced strong growth, with the church assuming the responsibility to meet the needs resulting from the breakdown of the educational system. The church became the schoolmaster of the South. In 1872, Dr. Thomas O. Sumners, editor of the *Nashville Christian Advocate*, wrote that three of the great Protestant communions—Baptist, Methodist, and Presbyterian—could educate all the children in the South. Other church leaders at this time predicted that the church would have a school wherever the Gospel is preached.

Presently, however, there is an undeniable shift in enrollment in institutions of higher learning to tax-supported schools. At the beginning of this century, 80 percent of all students were in private and church-related colleges and universities, and only 20 percent in tax-supported institutions. It is estimated that this figure will be reversed before the end of the century.

Many private colleges today are nondenominational or completely secular in nature. What they often have in common with the church-related colleges is that both are often rooted in Christian tradition. This tradition prevades the background and in varying degrees influences the character of private universities and colleges that are no longer church-related. Since today the approach to religion in these institutions differs so widely, in discussing the implications of the shift of enrollment to tax-supported institutions we shall limit our comments about private colleges and universities to those which are explicitly church-related. The Christian college not only has a religious program, it is a religious program. This distinction between *having* and *being* a religious program gives the reason for the existence of Christian institutions of higher learning.

State or municipal tax-supported institutions are not allowed to make comprehensive efforts to enhance the influence of religion on their campuses. They have courses in the history and theory of religion, but they lack the fundamental commitment and motivation that should pervade the Christian campus and make Christian faith relevant to any courses and programs offered on the campus. To be effective, religious education must have such relevance and not consist of pious but impractical religious pronouncements or formulas that have no meaning to those whom they are addressed. Such an educational program must not, however, abdicate its responsibility to the real world, nor attempt to dictate doctrinaire solutions.

In church-related colleges, since religion covers a wide range of beliefs and commitments, it is natural that controversies arise about whether certain activities are peripheral or whether they constitute the very core of the college's being. The Religious Emphasis Week, for instance, is disappearing from our major university campuses. Some may believe that the passing of this traditional event is an evidence of the decline of religious activities on our campuses. Others may argue that one week in a year cannot take the place of long-term commitment on the part of the church and that the demise of the Religious Emphasis Week witnesses rather to the increasing seriousness with which the church is taking its task to be of service to the life of the university.

There are those who strongly believe that frequent and regular attendance at the service in college chapel is required to demonstrate the nature of the Christian college, which calls for fellowship for both prayer and study. Others see in the conventional uses of the chapel service an oversimplification of the relationship between faith and higher education and point out the danger of forms becoming more important than substance.

The Christian college should serve as a forum for controversies involving religious issues. Such discussions lead to understanding that the college does not automatically become Christian by conducting a Religious Emphasis Week, building a chapel, or offering a number of religious courses. Structures and strategies of the campus ministry should be open to modification and change, be versatile and flexible, but always be directed toward the creation of an atmosphere of Christian concern that combines integrity of scholarship with love expressed in personal commitment, self-control, and acceptance of responsibility.

The church-related college is the church in education, in learning. Worship is the ground and reason for the college's existence only when combined with great, effective teaching. Intelligent Christian teaching must resist the danger of anti-intellectual pressure exercised by those who, in their lack of mature faith, try to shelter the students from the "modern" world. It must motivate the students to search for the truth, to find through creative thinking the purpose of life, and to discover the meaningfulness of the holy faith.

The support of church institutions of higher learning may depend upon ascertaining that the Christian college in its search for federal funding does not abdicate its responsibility to perform its duties in accordance with its fundamental commitment to studies that lead to understanding God's laws and discovery of God's truth. Supporters of Christian education may justly ask whether the church-related institution of higher learning performs its academic duties in the light of the Christian message or whether, in practice, it disassociates from the Christian basis on which it has been built.

Common Responsibility

The separation of church and State, the "wall of separation" concept under the establishment clause, does not permit public institutions to inculcate religious tenets or precepts in their students, but this does not mean that their students should not be made aware of the impact of moral standards offered by religion on our society. The recognition that religion is not solely a sectarian discipline, since it is concerned with human rights and the dignity of every individual, is the common responsibility of public as well as of private academic institutions. Thomas Jefferson outlined the necessity for all citizens to be aware of the questions raised by religious concern and of the various answers proposed for them:

> "The relations which exist between man and his Maker, and the duties resulting from those relations, are the most interesting and important to every human being, and the most incumbent on his study and investigation. The want of instruction in the various creeds of religious faith existing among our citizens presents, therefore, a chasm in a general institution of the useful sciences."

The separation of church and State does not imply that the State institution should be contemptuous of the commitment that calls for adherence to Christians' concepts of morality. Supreme Courts in various states, as we mentioned in Chapter I, have taken the position that Christian morality is the ethical code of the majority of the citizens furnishing "the purest system of morality, the firmest auxiliary, and only stable support of all human laws." *(Updegraph v. Commonwealth,* 11 Serg. § R [Pa.] 394 [1824]. See also for similar positions *State v. Chandler,* 2 Harr. [Del.] 533 [1839], and *People v. Ruggles,* 8 Johns. R [N.Y.] 290, 5 Am. Dec. 335 [1811].) The Supreme Court of the United States has held that the Bill of Rights recognizes "that in the domain of conscience there is a moral power higher than the State." *(Girouard v. United States,* 328 U.S. 61, 68 [1946].) The courts refer not to religion in its totality but to the Christian moral code which our law has adopted, recognizes, and embodies.

In more recent times the Supreme Court took the position that the State and religion are not required to be "aliens to each other—hostile, suspicious, and even unfriendly." It went on to say that "When the state encourages religious instruction or cooperates with religious authorities by adjusting the schedule of public events to sectarian needs, it follows the best of our traditions" and that "we find no constitutional requirement which makes it necessary for government to be hostile to religion and to throw its weight against efforts to widen the effective scope of religious influence." The Court gave specific recognition to the proposition that we "are a religious people whose institutions presuppose a Supreme Being." *(Zorach v. Clauson,* 343 U.S. 313-14 [1952].) The courts have also recognized that the Bible contains matters of great historical and literary value, as well as much moral instruction which is not in any sense sectarian. (68 Am. Jur. 2d 293.) In *Engel v. Vitale* (370 U.S. 421, 434 [1962]), the Court said: "The history of man is inseparable from the history of religions . . . And since the beginning of that history many people have devoutly believed that 'More things are wrought by prayer than this world dreams of.'"

The separation of church and State, under a democratic form of government, does not mean that the State should be the central agency of power and that the only source of absolute standards of right and wrong is in fact the State. By the same token the church should not be the central agency of power. The totalitarian church is as dangerous as the totalitarian State. Under totalitarianism, the dictator's couriers—the members of the political party in power, the State agencies, and the press—offer security to their country by proclaiming the infallibility of the dictator and by defying him. In their servility, they persuade citizens to praise if not glorify Hitler for revealing to them their racial superiority, Stalin for purging the "traitors," Khrushchev for crushing the revolution in Hungary, Brezhnev for invading Czechoslovakia or Afghanistan, or Khomeini for seizing the American embassy and holding American hostages.

Jeremiah warned against the false prophets who offer such security to their people: "They say still unto them that despise me, the Lord hath said, Ye shall have peace; and they say unto every one that walked after the imagination of his own heart, No evil shall come upon you." (Jeremiah 23:17.) The false prophets defy God's laws of life, which call for love, justice, and legality, and Jeremiah, in his great concern over this betrayal of God's laws, expresses his distress: "Mine heart within me is broken because of the prophets; all my bones shake." (23:9.)

Education for citizenship should foster freedom by pointing out the dangers of freeing the State to become its own god. The public confessions, forced by terror, to crimes never committed by political dissenters in communist countries remind us of the vivid story of the four hundred prophets in the first book of Kings. When Ahab, the King of Israel, asked Jehoshaphat, the King of Judah, to join him in a war against Ramoth-gilead, he gathered four hundred prophets who were attached to his court, and they unanimously delivered the prophetic verdict, "The Lord will deliver Ramoth-gilead into the hand of the king." (22:6.) Only the prophet Micaiah, when asked by messengers to maintain the unanimity of the four hundred prophets, replied, "As the Lord liveth, what the Lord saith unto me, that will I speak." (22:14.) When he painted the picture of the disaster which could be caused by the proposed war, the King of Israel banished him to prison.

The divinization of the State substitutes absolute nothingness for an absolute, fundamental conception of values. Arthur Koestler makes this point in his novel, *Darkness at Noon*, when he has his character Rubashov say in his manipulated confession:

> "If I ask myself to-day, 'For what am I dying?' I am confronted by absolute nothingness. There is nothing for which one could die, if one died with-

out having repented and unreconciled with the Party and the Movement. Therefore, on the threshold of my last hour, I bend my knees to the country, to the masses and to the whole people. The political masquerade, the mummery of discussions and conspiracy are over. We were politically dead long before the Citizen prosecutor demanded our heads. Woe unto the defeated, whom history treads into the dust." (Koestler, *Darkness at Noon*, Macmillan, 1941, p. 251.)

Throughout the history of mankind there has been an ongoing search for absolute moral values, for the absolute laws which Cicero described as *Lex ad quam non eruditi sumus sed nati sumus*—the laws to which we are born and not trained. Hammurabi, Moses, Confucius, the Greek philosophers, the Roman jurists and statesmen, the philosophers and scientists who molded our modern civilization— they all looked for fundamental moral values imbedded in all phases of the development of civilization, whether they like Aristotle considered that "the state or political community . . . is the highest good of all" or like St. Augustine, who by identifying the church with the kingdom of God and by claiming divinity for this human institution, saw the church as the highest active force for social justice.

Public educational institutions cannot divorce themselves from the fact that Christianity has entered and influenced, more or less, all our institutions, customs, and relations, as well as all our individual modes of thinking and acting. "It is involved in our social nature, that even those among us who reject Christianity, cannot possibly get clear of its influence, or reject those sentiments, customs and principles which it has spread among the people, so that, like the air we breathe, they have become the common stock of the whole country, and essential elements of its life." (*Mohney v. Cook*, 26 Pa. 342 [1855].)

Among the traditions of our nation in which religion has become intertwined with government are chaplains in both Houses of Congress, chaplains in all branches of the Armed Forces, compulsory chapel at the military service academies, the use of the Bible for oaths, religious proclamations by the President, the reference to God on coins and in the pledge of allegiance, exemption of religious organizations from taxation, and deduction of religious donations for income tax purposes.

The common responsibility of public and private academic institutions—the inquiring conscience of society—is to provide the student with a conception of what it means to be a free man and with stable standards of moral judgment. No educational institution should become a political instrument or the obliging servant of any political or economic group. Alongside intellectual discipline and scientific study, it has to fulfill the express purpose of building character upon the foundation of moral principles. Its sacred task is to combine the love of learning with the citizen's allegiance to his community. The concern for virtues and spiritual values is the very core of the existence of academic institutions whether public, private, or church-related. They are committed to develop persons of strong moral character who would serve their fellowman. They are commited to share convictions strongly rooted in their heritage of leadership that comes from within the institution and is reflected in the entire pattern of learning and campus life.

Without the general direction of the moral code calling for service to our fellowman, human society becomes aimless and meaningless, and pursuit of pleasure that weakens its spiritual fiber takes the place of the pursuit of happiness guaranteed by the Declaration of Independence. A society in which rights to pesonal gratification and well-being are stressed without correlating them with obligations to one's fellowman and one's country cannot survive.

In order to avoid generalities, we would like to cite a few examples of how knowledge supplemented by moral principles creates a climate out of which commitment to service may emerge in such varied disciplines as medicine, law, economics, and the sciences. Moral and spiritual fiber may not substitute for medical skill, but it may induce students of medicine to give their lives on the altar of service of mankind in search of means for delivering man from the sufferings that beset him. Albert Schweitzer pointed out that his determination to become a medical missionary stemmed from the growing understanding within himself of Jesus' message that we must not treat our lives as being for ourselves alone and that "whoever is spared personal pain must feel himself called to help in diminishing the pain of others." (*Out of My Life and Thought*, Henry Holt, 1933, pp. 81-82.)

In the law schools, in addition to the study of manmade statutes, rules, court decisions, and administrative regulations, there should be a constant search for moral order. In the words of Reinhold Niebuhr, "The cure for modern lawlessness is not more emphasis upon law or efforts to define specific laws more sharply. The cure for modern lawlessness is to bring the idolatry and self-worship of all men and nations under divine judgement ..." (*Man's Disorder and God's Design*, Amsterdam Assembly Series, Volume III, Harper Brothers, p. 27.) The principles found in Leviticus, "In righteousness shall you judge your neighbor" (19:15), and expressed by Paul, "Love cannot wrong a neighbor; therefore, the whole law is summed up in love" (Romans 13:10), constitute the very framework of the administration of justice.

Man's giant strides in knowledge and control of his natural environment, his trust and dependence on the power of science also put in his hands the power of annihilation of the human race. It is the responsibility of education for citizenship to inspire an apathetic world and to renew the affirmation of the rule of law, the only instrument strong enough to forestall this annihilation. No society can endure without order and due process. (Romans 13:1-7.) Respect for the rule of law creates no conflict with the right of legal redress and of dissent. The integrity of our administration of justice depends upon its vivid response to warranted complaints of injustice and inequity. The sufferings of the early Christians are constant reminders of the importance of rights to free speech and peaceful assembly.

Nor can an educated citizen be complacent in the face of economic exploitations and inequalities of wealth when multitudes are sick of poverty and hunger. In socialistic countries, the attempts to eliminate inequalities in wealth result in making everyone poor. This is not the equality we seek. Inequalities that do not endanger the well-being of society, and do not tend to destroy fellowship, must be accepted, provided that every citizen has the right to equal opportunities through equal access to education and employment.

There is a need for the incentive and initiative of every citizen who has not only the right but also the obligation to work and through work to serve the communtiy. Work should minister to the worker's spiritual welfare as well as to the community's welfare. There is no Christian physics, mathematics, or botany. As Harold C. Case, President of Boston University, has pointed out, "When a Christian teacher imparts his knowledge of mathematics or botany to his student, his faith adds overtones so that the same subject matter has an inspiring glow and deeper meaning." This faith enhances what the French philosopher Jean-Jacques Rousseau observes—the inner nobility of man.

Education for World Citizenship

In my book *The Third Way*, I defined a Christian world citizen as a "patriot who exerts himself to promote the welfare of his country, ready to defend it against open or subversive aggression, but who, at the same time, is concerned about the welfare of other nations and with compassion is ready to share his fellowman's destiny." (*The Third Way*, p. 131.)

In the Old Testament, the early Hebrews claimed a peculiar relationship to God as his chosen people. But the prophets saw God's love as transcending national boundaries and his concern as extending to the destinies of other peoples besides his own. Amos asks: "Are ye not as children of the Ethiopians unto me, children of Israel? saith the Lord. Have not I brought up Israel out of the land of Egypt? and the Philistines from Caphtor, and the Syrians form Kir?" (Amos 9:7.)

The Hebrews are not the only nation who have needed such reminders. We too, like other nations, have sometimes subscribed to the unconscious ideal of a national god while pretending to call upon and worship the eternal and universal God. In times of war, men in opposing camps characteristically invoke the aid of "their" God, and troops are sent into the battlefield in the belief that God is "on their side." During the time of our own Civil War, Lincoln noted this anomaly, saying of the North and South that "Both read the same Bible and pray to the same God, and each invokes his aid against the other. The prayers of both could not be answered." And again in his Second Inaugural Address he noted, "It seems strange that men should ask the assistance of God in wringing their bread from other men's toil."

The eternal and universal God is not an ally of any one nation engaged in battle. As Niebuhr pointed out, this is why in the first book of Chronicles God said to David, "Thou shalt not build an house for my name, because thou hast been a man of war and hast shed blood . . . Solomon thy son, he shall build my house and my courts . . ." (I Chronicles 28:3, 6, as quoted in Niebuhr, *Beyond Tragedy*, p. 48.) The true vision of the eternal and universal God leads in turn to a vision of sacred brotherhood, "with malice toward none, with charity toward all," and recognizes that the gospel passage "God so loved the *world* that he gave his only-begotten Son" (John 3:15) cannot be limited in its application to any one country or people.

Because of our obligations to our fellowman throughout the world, an essential component of education for citizenship is training young people for service in underdeveloped areas throughout the world. It is vital that we demonstrate the principles of world citizenship by both word and deeds and that our interest in the well-being of people of underdeveloped nations be free from any design to exploit or oppress them or to seek any special privileges. To be effective in teaching the people living under subnormal conditions our know-how, its application in modern industry and agriculture, and how our scientific advancement might be used efficaciously— we must win the friendship and confidence of the peoples of underdeveloped areas.

How can we win the confidence of the peoples of underdeveloped areas? First, we must recognize the meaning and values of *patience.* In our program for underdeveloped countries we must be prepared for rocky enterprises. With technological backwardness in many countries are preserved archaic land relations and, what is worse, ignorance and superstition. The trust in progress will come when people become convinced that someone is trying to share with them the God-given human rights to which they are entitled.

Second, the knowledge of the native language has fundamental implications in the course of human relations. In the sixteenth century the British philosopher Francis Bacon wrote, "He that travelleth into a country before he has some entrance into the language, goeth to school, and not to travel." Friendship is a "plant of slow growth," and the knowledge of the language of our neighbors gives the great opportunity to find an accord in our common affairs and to eliminate the seeds of suspicion in the minds of the natives of the underdeveloped countries. The friendliness which we try to offer is often seriously discounted by the incorrect usage or non-usage of their language. Training in foreign languages has been proved to break down the communication barrier and to lead to understanding and respect of the culture and customs of the native world.

The exclusiveness of foreigners' residential "colonies" or enclaves can also in no way be considered as a contribution to our friendship with the peoples of underdeveloped countries. Representatives of industrialized countries living abroad often confine their social contacts mostly to themselves. Such self-insulated walls exclude association with new friends, and this attitude is generally interpreted as egotism and wounds those sensitively searching for equality. The local citizens know that their countries are underdeveloped. Their recognition of this fact is one of the chief reasons why the way we deal with them attracts special attention. Their national, or merely human, pride is offended when we are indifferent to their traditions and customs. It is important that the foreign technician, businessman, or missionary take an interest in the new culture in which he lives, reading books and magazines other than in his native language, making friends with others than those of his own cultural group.

Third, we must stress the meaning and value of modesty. The underdeveloped countries are areas in which income is very low and distribution of income results in fundamental injustices. The people under the prevailing system of oligarchy or dictatorship are not able to secure their necessities. We have therefore to remember that poverty breeds strife and that envy is a human passion which, according to La Rochefoucauld, is more irreconcilable than hatred. "Wrath is cruel, and anger is outrageous, but who is able to stand before envy?" (Proverbs 27:4.)

We cannot expect our friends in underdeveloped areas to admire without envy our good fortune and our high standards of living. Confucius once wrote: "It is harder to be poor without murmuring than to be rich without arrogance." There is the undercurrent of hostility of the poor and hungry toward those who possess and enjoy abundance and plenty. The Spanish proverb says: *Quien ha criados ha enemigos no escusados* (he who has servants has unavoidable enemies).

Fourth, there is one more factor that should be taken into consideration. In underdeveloped countries we can find the economic power concentrated in the hands of a few, who live in luxury unknown even in the United States. They often use the campaign against the American engineer, businessman, or teacher, who lives much more comfortably than the starving miner or factory worker, as a handy way of diverting attention from domestic injustices. The "spirit" of this type of campaign explains the hostile attitude toward the foreigners in some of the under-developed countries. The truth is that in order to give a living example of world citizenship we cannot be complacent in the face of economic exploitation and inequalities of wealth when multitudes are sick and tired of poverty, famine, and hunger.

In spite of the opposition to "foreign millionaires," the people of the underdeveloped countries realize the work done for them not only in the field of religion, but in public health, social service, and education. Great care must be taken in recruiting the right type of personnel for such activities and in giving them special training in the culture and the needs of the areas to which they go. The sooner we carry out our task of helping the peoples of the underdeveloped areas, the better are the hopes for a free world. A large part of the unrest in the Third World results from an upsurge of the people who have long suffered in poverty and misrule.

Arnold J. Toynbee, one of the great twentieth-century historians, concluding his address on "Man at Work in God's World," delivered before the Church and Work Congress, stated:

> "My first point is that Man's Work in God's World cannot be healthy or beneficent unless we consecrate it . . . My second point is that the price of consecration is the same as the price of liberty: it is eternal vigilance—and the exercise of this vigilance cannot be delegated by you and me to the public authorities, civil or ecclesiastical, for them

192 THE FOUNDATIONS OF A FREE SOCIETY

to administer it for us vicariously. This is not feasible, because the place where Work is consecrated is not the impersonal field of relations between us which we call Society; the place where Work goes right or wrong is the soul of each individual human being . . ." (*Vital Speeches*, Volume XXII, No. 3, p. 96.)

The signers of the Declaration of Independence pledged their lives, fortunes, and sacred honor. "Sacred honor"is embodied in the conception of entire surrender to the will of God. Such surrender provides a spiritual force which will lend purpose to the task of efficient government and citizenship. Supported by this force, the emotionally and intellectually mature citizen will have the ability to relate his talents to continuing progress of the society in which he lives. "None of us lives to himself, and none of us dies to himself." (Romans 14:7.)